# It's another Quality Book from CGP

This book is for 7-11 year olds.

Whatever subject you're doing it's the same
old story — there are lots of facts and you've just got
to learn them. KS2 Maths is no different.

Happily this CGP book gives you all that important
information as clearly and concisely as possible.

It's also got some daft bits in to try and make the whole
experience at least vaguely entertaining for you.

# What CGP is all about

Our sole aim here at CGP is to produce the highest quality
books — carefully written, immaculately presented and
dangerously close to being funny.

Then we work our socks off to get them out to you
— at the cheapest possible prices.

# Contents

## SECTION ONE — NUMBERS

Number Stuff ............................................................................ 1
Adding Without a Calculator ................................................. 5
Subtracting Without a Calculator ......................................... 7
Negative Numbers .................................................................. 9
Multiplication ......................................................................... 12
Multiplication Without a Calculator ..................................... 13
Division .................................................................................... 15
Division Without a Calculator ............................................... 16
Typical Questions ................................................................... 19
Decimals .................................................................................. 21
Rounding Off ........................................................................... 23
Mental Arithmetic .................................................................. 25
Calculations With Money ....................................................... 29
Practice Questions ................................................................. 31

## SECTION TWO — MORE NUMBER STUFF

Calculators .............................................................................. 32
Fractions .................................................................................. 33
Division and Fractions ........................................................... 37
Percentages ............................................................................. 38
Estimating Fractions and Percentages ................................ 41
Ratio and Proportion .............................................................. 42
Multiples .................................................................................. 43
Factors ..................................................................................... 44
Prime Numbers ....................................................................... 45
Prime Factors .......................................................................... 46
Even and Odd Numbers ......................................................... 47
Square Numbers ..................................................................... 48
Calculators (2) ........................................................................ 49
Number Patterns and Sequences ......................................... 50
Word Formulae and Equations .............................................. 54
Function Machines .................................................................. 56
Practice Questions ................................................................. 57

# SECTION THREE — SHAPES AND SOLIDS

Angles ................................................................ 58
The Shapes You Need to Know ............................... 60
Perimeters ........................................................... 62
Areas .................................................................. 64
Congruence .......................................................... 66
Symmetry ............................................................ 67
Reflection, Translation and Rotation ....................... 69
3-D Shapes You Need to Know ............................... 72
Shape Nets .......................................................... 73
Practice Questions ............................................... 75

# SECTION FOUR — MEASUREMENT

Plotting Coordinates ............................................ 76
Time ................................................................... 77
Timetables .......................................................... 79
Units .................................................................. 80
Conversions ......................................................... 83
Reading Scales ..................................................... 85
Maps and Compass Directions ............................... 87
Practice Questions ............................................... 88

# SECTION FIVE — HANDLING DATA

Tables ................................................................. 89
Tally Marks .......................................................... 90
Bar Charts ........................................................... 91
Pictograms .......................................................... 93
Line Graphs ......................................................... 94
Pie Charts ........................................................... 96
Mean, Median, Mode and Range ............................ 98
Probability ......................................................... 101
Practice Questions ............................................. 102

Some Words You Need to Know ............................. 103
Answers ............................................................. 104
Index ................................................................. 106

Published by CGP
Illustrated by Lex Ward and Ashley Tyson

*Contributors:*
Ruso Bradley
Paul Jordin
Sharon Keeley
Simon Little
Chris Oates
Glenn Rogers
Claire Thompson
Tim Wakeling

ISBN: 978 1 84762 184 9

Groovy website: www.cgpbooks.co.uk
Printed by Elanders Ltd, Newcastle upon Tyne.
Clipart sources: CorelDRAW® and VECTOR.

Based on the classic CGP style created by Richard Parsons.

# Number Stuff

## All Numbers are Made of Digits

1) A digit is just one of these: 0 1 2 3 4 5 6 7 8 9
2) We stick them together to write bigger numbers.
3) 10, 23, 57 are <u>two-digit</u> numbers. 1112, 2745, 6473 are <u>four-digit</u> numbers.
4) The <u>position</u> of a digit in a number is important. Its value depends upon its position in the number. Think of each digit as being in a <u>separate box</u>.
5) Each box is worth <u>10 times as much</u> as the box to its right.

| Hundreds | Tens | Units |
|---|---|---|
| 2 | 4 | 1 |

e.g. Look at the number **241**

The value of the digit 2 is <u>two hundred</u>.
The value of the digit 4 is four tens, or <u>forty</u>.

| Hundred (Thousands) | Ten (Thousands) | Unit (Thousands) | Hundreds | Tens | Units |
|---|---|---|---|---|---|
| | 9 | 9 | 9 | 9 | 9 |
| 1 | 0 | 0 | 0 | 0 | 0 |

100 000 is bigger than 99 999...

...because it fills a box <u>further to the left</u>.

## Writing Numbers in Words

**EXAMPLE:**  Write 37 in words.

Two-digit numbers are easy, just write them like you would say them — so it's "thirty-seven".

**EXAMPLE:**  Write 437 in words.

For three-digit numbers just write the number of hundreds, then "and", then the tens and units just like this:

"Four hundred and thirty-seven".  (Always say "hundred" not "hundreds".)

**EXAMPLE:**  Write 23437 in words.

This is the number of <u>thousands</u> ie "<u>twenty-three</u>" of them.

## 23 437

And this is the rest.
"<u>Four hundred and thirty-seven</u>".

### The Method

1) Stick a space in it <u>3 DIGITS FROM THE RIGHT</u> (to separate the thousands bit from the rest).
2) Treat it like <u>2 SEPARATE NUMBERS</u>.
3) The <u>Thousand</u> bit comes first.
4) Next come the hundreds, tens and units.

So we write this "twenty-three thousand, four hundred and thirty-seven".

# Number Stuff

## Counting on in 10s and 100s

This is just like normal counting, except you increase the tens digit or the hundreds digit instead of the units digit.

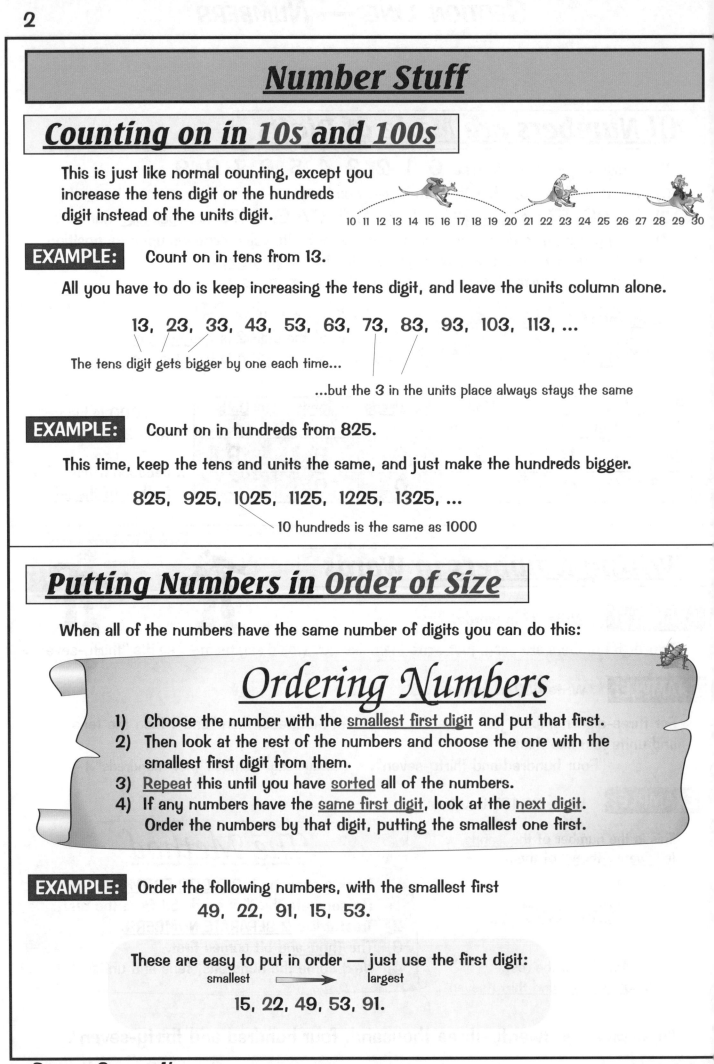

10 11 12 13 14 15 16 17 18 19 20 21 22 23 24 25 26 27 28 29 30

**EXAMPLE:** Count on in tens from 13.

All you have to do is keep increasing the tens digit, and leave the units column alone.

13, 23, 33, 43, 53, 63, 73, 83, 93, 103, 113, ...

The tens digit gets bigger by one each time...

...but the 3 in the units place always stays the same

**EXAMPLE:** Count on in hundreds from 825.

This time, keep the tens and units the same, and just make the hundreds bigger.

825, 925, 1025, 1125, 1225, 1325, ...

10 hundreds is the same as 1000

## Putting Numbers in Order of Size

When all of the numbers have the same number of digits you can do this:

### Ordering Numbers

1) Choose the number with the <u>smallest first digit</u> and put that first.
2) Then look at the rest of the numbers and choose the one with the smallest first digit from them.
3) <u>Repeat</u> this until you have <u>sorted</u> all of the numbers.
4) If any numbers have the <u>same first digit</u>, look at the <u>next digit</u>. Order the numbers by that digit, putting the smallest one first.

**EXAMPLE:** Order the following numbers, with the smallest first

49, 22, 91, 15, 53.

These are easy to put in order — just use the first digit:

smallest ➡ largest

15, 22, 49, 53, 91.

# Number Stuff

**EXAMPLE:** Order the following numbers, with the smallest first
184, 967, 495, 332, 325.

1) Order by the leftmost digit:

smallest ⟶ largest

184, 332, 325 , 495, 967.

Same digit – so look at
the next digit to the right.

2) Order by the next digit along:

332, 325

3 is bigger than 2, so
swap the numbers around.

3) So the correct order is:

184, 325, 332, 495, 967.

Order.
Order.

**DON'T FORGET:**
You can only do this when <u>all</u>
the numbers have the <u>same</u>
<u>number</u> of digits.

---

**EXAMPLE:** Order the numbers 3491, 3272, 3284, 3291.

Yuk! They all look horrible. But it's still dead easy if you just follow the method.

1) Order by the leftmost digit:

<u>3</u>491, <u>3</u>291, <u>3</u>284, <u>3</u>272

They're all the same, so that was no help.
Okay then — look at the next digits along.

2) 3<u>2</u>91, 3<u>2</u>84, 3<u>2</u>72, 3491.

Well this one's in the right place now.

Go onto the third digit for these three.

3) Onto the third digit:

3272, 3284, 3291. And that's it.

4) So the correct order is:

3272, 3284, 3291, 3491.

# Number Stuff

**EXAMPLE:** 49    220    13    3402    76    94    105    684

This time they don't all have the same number of digits. That's no problem — we just sort them into groups first.

1) Put them into groups, the ones with the <u>fewest digits first</u>.

| 49  13  76  94 | 220  105  684 | 3402 |
|---|---|---|
| 2 digits | 3 digits | 4 digits |

2) For each separate group put them in <u>order of size</u>. (Just like we did before.)

| 13  49  76  94 | 105  220  684 | 3402 |
|---|---|---|

**EXAMPLE:** Arrange the digits 4, 7, 3 and 2 to make the smallest possible number.

1) Put the digits in <u>order</u> with the <u>smallest first</u>.     2, 3, 4, 7
2) Stick them together to form the number.     So the number is 2347

You also need to know the <u>signs</u> for <u>comparing</u> numbers:

> means <u>greater than</u> and < means <u>less than</u>

**EXAMPLES:** "a > 5" means "<u>a is greater than 5</u>",     "b < 3" means "<u>b is less than 3</u>".

# Noughts are Important

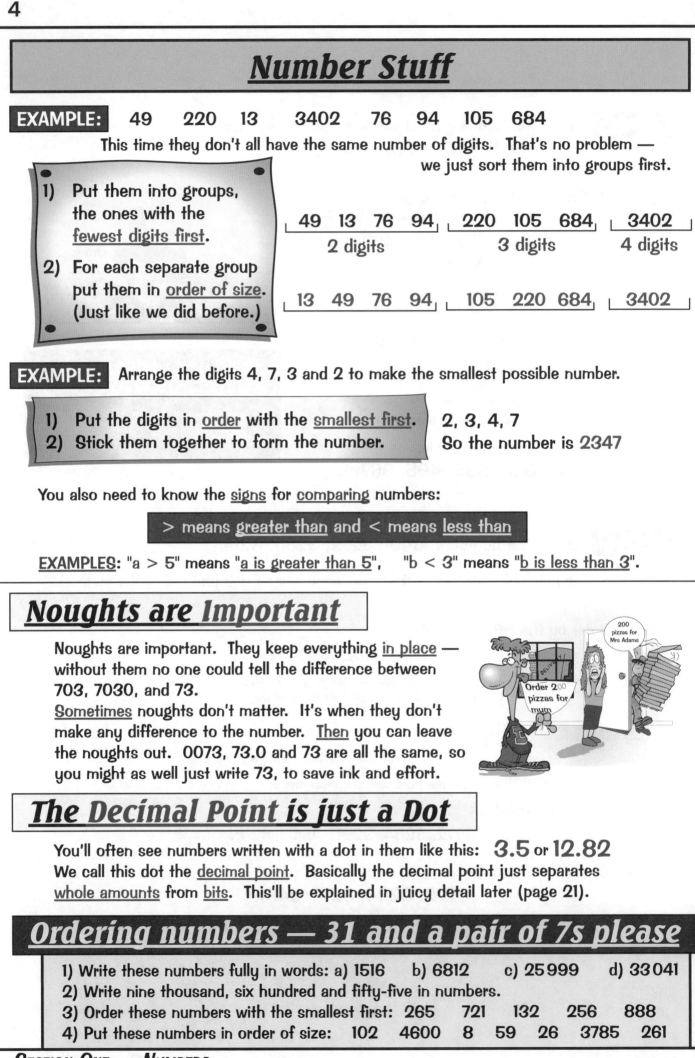

Noughts are important. They keep everything <u>in place</u> — without them no one could tell the difference between 703, 7030, and 73.
<u>Sometimes</u> noughts don't matter. It's when they don't make any difference to the number. <u>Then</u> you can leave the noughts out. 0073, 73.0 and 73 are all the same, so you might as well just write 73, to save ink and effort.

# The Decimal Point is just a Dot

You'll often see numbers written with a dot in them like this: **3.5** or **12.82**
We call this dot the <u>decimal point</u>. Basically the decimal point just separates <u>whole amounts</u> from <u>bits</u>. This'll be explained in juicy detail later (page 21).

# Ordering numbers — 31 and a pair of 7s please

1) Write these numbers fully in words: a) 1516     b) 6812     c) 25 999     d) 33 041
2) Write nine thousand, six hundred and fifty-five in numbers.
3) Order these numbers with the smallest first: 265     721     132     256     888
4) Put these numbers in order of size:    102    4600    8    59    26    3785    261

# Adding Without a Calculator

This sort of stuff is really important and you're bound to get tested on it. It may seem a bit tricky at first but once you get the knack it's not too bad.

no calculators!!

## Adding Numbers

### Adding Numbers

1) Write the numbers one on top of the other with the underlined units lined up.
2) Add the Units column first, then the Tens, then the Hundreds.
3) If one of the columns adds to an answer of 10 or more,
   - put the right digit of the answer in that column, and
   - carry the left digit to the column on the left.

**EXAMPLE:** Work out 681 + 556 without using a calculator.

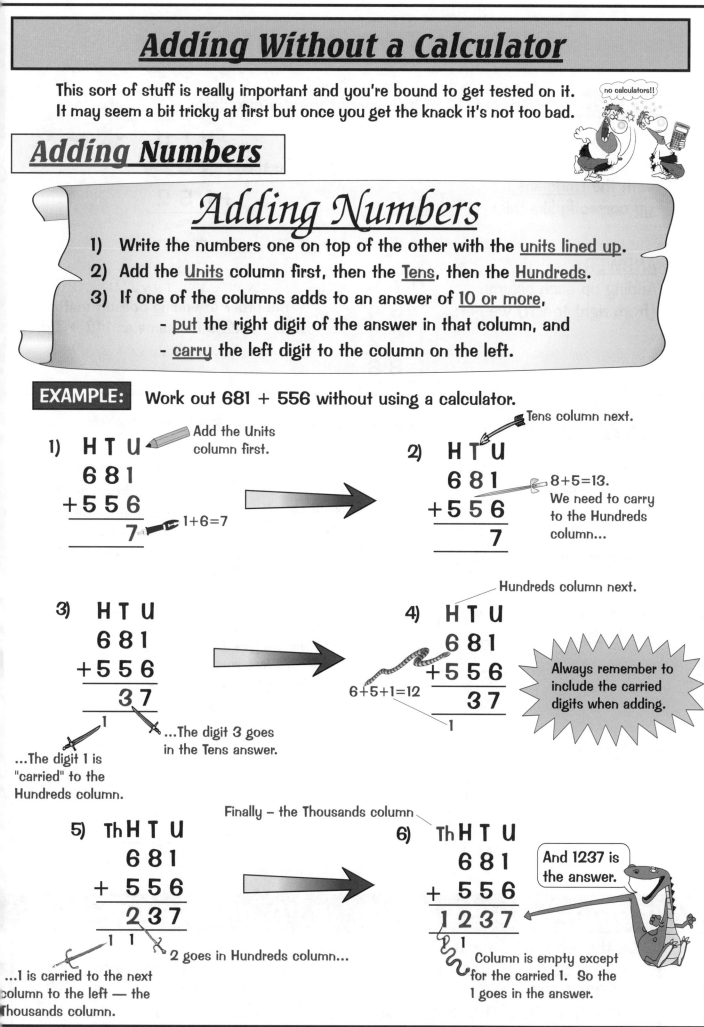

1) Add the Units column first.

```
 H T U
 6 8 1
+5 5 6
------
     7
```
1+6=7

2) Tens column next.
```
 H T U
 6 8 1
+5 5 6
------
     7
```
8+5=13. We need to carry to the Hundreds column...

3)
```
 H T U
 6 8 1
+5 5 6
------
   3 7
     1
```
...The digit 3 goes in the Tens answer.
...The digit 1 is "carried" to the Hundreds column.

4) Hundreds column next.
```
 H T U
 6 8 1
+5 5 6
------
   3 7
   1
```
6+5+1=12

Always remember to include the carried digits when adding.

5)
```
Th H T U
   6 8 1
 + 5 5 6
--------
   2 3 7
   1 1
```
2 goes in Hundreds column...
...1 is carried to the next column to the left — the Thousands column.

6) Finally – the Thousands column
```
Th H T U
   6 8 1
 + 5 5 6
--------
 1 2 3 7
   1
```
And 1237 is the answer.
Column is empty except for the carried 1. So the 1 goes in the answer.

# Adding Without a Calculator

**EXAMPLE:** Work out 34 + 152 without using a calculator.

This one's easy as long as you write it with the <u>Units lined up</u> correctly like this:

```
H T U
  3 4
+1 5 2
_____
```

and <u>NOT</u> like this:

```
H T U
3 4
+1 5 2
_____
```

<u>ANSWER:</u>
Adding up each column (from right to left) we get:

```
H T U
  3 4
+1 5 2
_____
1 8 6
```

The order of adding doesn't matter
243 + 142 is the same as 142 + 243

**EXAMPLE:** Find the missing digits in the sum 3☐2 + 55☐ = 915

1) As usual, start with the <u>Units</u>, then do the Tens and so on.

```
H T U
3 ☐ 2
+ 5 5 ☐
_____
9 1 5
```

2 plus something is 5.
Easy: 2+3=5,
so 3 goes here.

They're very keen on this sort of question in the tests. So it's a good idea to get some practice in on them.

2) Now look at the <u>Tens</u>.

```
H T U
3 ☐ 2
+ 5 5 ③
_____
9 1 5
```

We can't add anything to 5 to get 1.
<u>But</u>: 6+5=11. This will give the 1
we need for the Tens answer.
(The other 1 digit is carried to the H column.)

3) <u>Check</u> that the H column works.

```
H T U
3 ⑥ 2
+ 5 5 ③
_____
9 1 5
1
```

3+5+1=9
So it works.

The carried 1 from the Tens column.

At the end, add up the numbers to <u>CHECK</u> that they give the right answer.

# Adding — that's the noise my doorbell makes...

Do the following without using a calculator:
1) 13 + 25        2) 64 + 35        3) 164 + 12        4) 286 + 46
5) 325 + 87       6) 123 + 112      7) 364 + 274       8) 687 + 272
9) 586 + 596      10) 294 + 889     11) 1425 + 213     12) 1052 + 1523

# Subtracting Without a Calculator

Subtraction is just "taking away". In questions, if they ask you to "find the difference" they mean subtract the smaller number from the bigger number.

## Subtracting is Taking Away

**EXAMPLE:** Find the difference between 162 and 435.

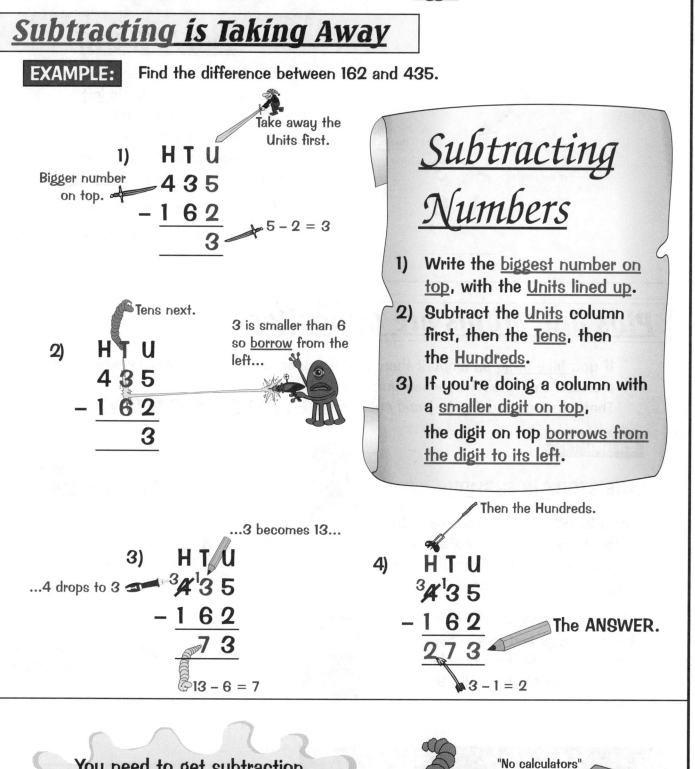

Take away the Units first.

1)
```
  H T U
Bigger number →  4 3 5
on top.      - 1 6 2
                  3
```
5 − 2 = 3

### Subtracting Numbers

1) Write the **biggest number on top**, with the Units lined up.

2) Subtract the **Units** column first, then the **Tens**, then the **Hundreds**.

3) If you're doing a column with a **smaller digit on top**, the digit on top **borrows from the digit to its left**.

Tens next.

3 is smaller than 6 so borrow from the left...

2)
```
  H T U
  4 3 5
- 1 6 2
      3
```

...3 becomes 13...

3)
```
   H T U
...4 drops to 3    ³4̶ ¹3 5
        - 1 6 2
            7 3
```
13 − 6 = 7

Then the Hundreds.

4)
```
  H T U
  ³4̶ ¹3 5
- 1 6 2
  2 7 3
```
The ANSWER.

3 − 1 = 2

You need to get subtraction the right way round:
68 − 55 is not the same as 55 − 68

"No calculators"

# *Subtracting Without a Calculator*

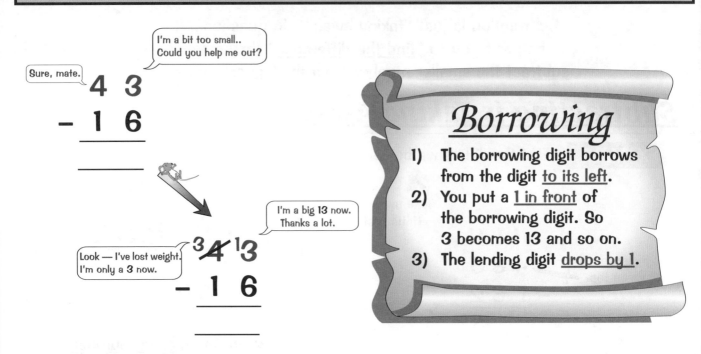

I'm a bit too small..
Could you help me out?

Sure, mate.

$$4 \quad 3$$
$$- \quad 1 \quad 6$$

I'm a big **13** now.
Thanks a lot.

Look — I've lost weight.
I'm only a **3** now.

$$^3\!\!\!\!\backslash\!4 \; ^1\!3$$
$$- \quad 1 \quad 6$$

## *Borrowing*

1) The borrowing digit borrows from the digit <u>to its left</u>.
2) You put a <u>1 in front</u> of the borrowing digit. So 3 becomes 13 and so on.
3) The lending digit <u>drops by 1</u>.

## *Plus and Minus are Opposites*

If you <u>take away</u> an amount then <u>add</u> the same amount, you're back where you started. Pretty obvious when you say it.

That's because adding (+) and subtracting (−) <u>DO THE OPPOSITE THING</u>.

### EXAMPLE:

**THE STORY IN <u>ENGLISH</u>:**

Mr Oddbod is a bug collector, with a total of 96 bugs in his collection. He buys 4 new ones from the local bug fair, so he now has 100.

His wife doesn't like the look of the new bugs and makes him return them. So he's now left with what he started with, 96 normal bugs.

**THE STORY IN <u>MATHS</u>:**

$$96 + 4 = 100$$

$$100 - 4 = 96$$

## *Taking — the King of Ta*

Do the following without using a calculator:

1) 33 − 24  2) 75 − 27  3) 164 − 13  4) 785 − 46
5) 584 − 87  6) 189 − 113  7) 987 − 472  8) 935 − 119
9) Find the difference between:  a) 12 and 95  b) 192 and 113  c) 263 and 956

# Negative Numbers

Sometimes we need to use numbers <u>less than zero</u>. We call them <u>negative numbers</u>, and write them with a minus sign in front.

## Negative Numbers — Where do they Come From?

Negative numbers pop up in all sorts of places. We use them for cold temperatures like -5°C (minus five degrees Celsius).

If you have -£10.00 in the bank, then it means you <u>owe</u> the bank £10 (a shame really).

## The Number Line

The <u>number line</u> is really useful for understanding negative numbers.

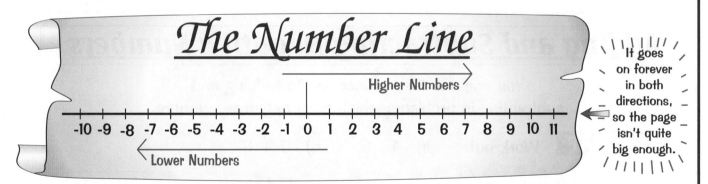

It's like a huge thermometer scale that goes on forever in both directions. It has every number on it in the correct order. The further right you go, the higher the numbers get. The further left, the lower the numbers. Notice that:

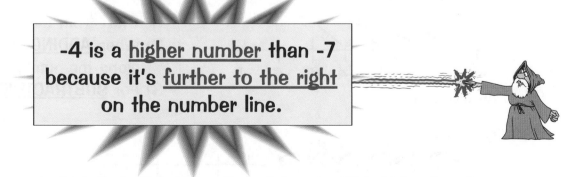

-4 is a <u>higher number</u> than -7 because it's <u>further to the right</u> on the number line.

It's easy to think that -10 is higher than -6 because 10 is higher than 6. But check the number line and you'll see that it's not.

# Negative Numbers

## Putting Negative Numbers in Order

### Ordering Negative Numbers

1) Quickly <u>draw</u> part of the number line (with the right numbers on).

2) Put the numbers in the <u>same order</u> as they appear on the number line.

*They're going to get it wrong. I just know it.*

*Don't be so negative.*

**EXAMPLE:** Put these in order of size: -4, 5, -2, 10, -9, 2, -7.

<u>ANSWER:</u>

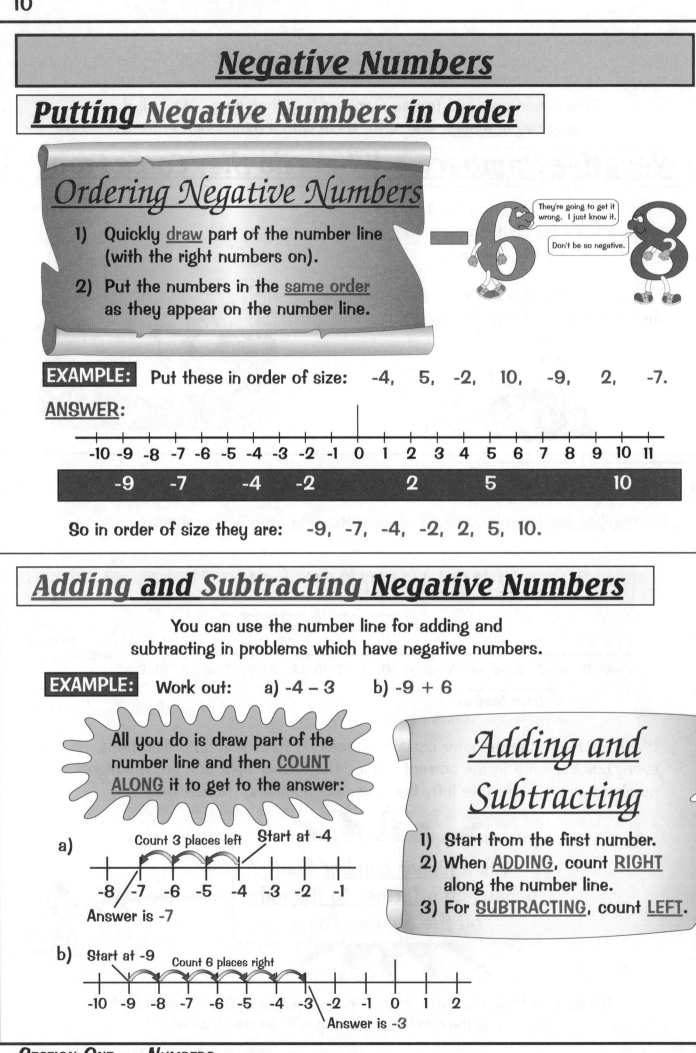

-10 -9 -8 -7 -6 -5 -4 -3 -2 -1 0 1 2 3 4 5 6 7 8 9 10 11

-9  -7  -4  -2  2  5  10

So in order of size they are: -9, -7, -4, -2, 2, 5, 10.

## Adding and Subtracting Negative Numbers

You can use the number line for adding and subtracting in problems which have negative numbers.

**EXAMPLE:** Work out: a) -4 – 3 b) -9 + 6

All you do is draw part of the number line and then <u>COUNT ALONG</u> it to get to the answer:

### Adding and Subtracting

1) Start from the first number.
2) When <u>ADDING</u>, count <u>RIGHT</u> along the number line.
3) For <u>SUBTRACTING</u>, count <u>LEFT</u>.

a)

Count 3 places left   Start at -4

-8 -7 -6 -5 -4 -3 -2 -1

Answer is -7

b)   Start at -9   Count 6 places right

-10 -9 -8 -7 -6 -5 -4 -3 -2 -1 0 1 2

Answer is -3

# Negative Numbers

## Working Out Temperature Changes

Test questions often ask about changes in
TEMPERATURE — especially for places
where it goes below freezing at night.

*My thermometer keeps dropping.*

*Nail it to the wall then.*

**EXAMPLE:** One day the temperature in Neil's freezer was -15°C, but it rose to 7°C after he filled it with fermenting cheesecakes. What was the <u>rise</u> in temperature?

<u>ANSWER</u>: Once again, just do a quick sketch of the number line, mark the two temperatures on it and then just <u>count how many degrees</u> it is between them:

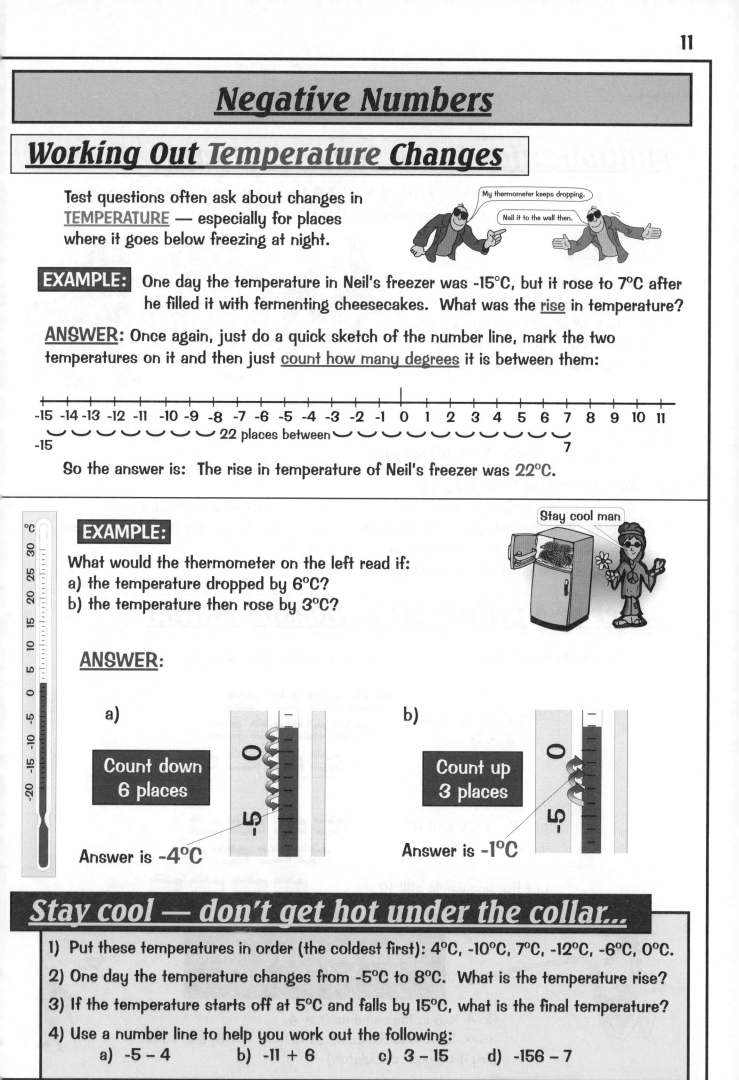

-15 -14 -13 -12 -11 -10 -9 -8 -7 -6 -5 -4 -3 -2 -1 0 1 2 3 4 5 6 7 8 9 10 11

22 places between

-15                                                                 7

So the answer is: The rise in temperature of Neil's freezer was **22°C**.

**EXAMPLE:**

*Stay cool man*

What would the thermometer on the left read if:
a) the temperature dropped by 6°C?
b) the temperature then rose by 3°C?

<u>ANSWER</u>:

a)

**Count down
6 places**

Answer is **-4°C**

b)

**Count up
3 places**

Answer is **-1°C**

## Stay cool — don't get hot under the collar...

1) Put these temperatures in order (the coldest first): 4°C, -10°C, 7°C, -12°C, -6°C, 0°C.

2) One day the temperature changes from -5°C to 8°C. What is the temperature rise?

3) If the temperature starts off at 5°C and falls by 15°C, what is the final temperature?

4) Use a number line to help you work out the following:
    a) -5 – 4        b) -11 + 6        c) 3 – 15        d) -156 – 7

# Multiplication

## Multiplication is the Same as "Times"

If we had to find out how many <u>5 lots of 23</u> is, we'd work out "<u>5 times 23</u>".
The fancy word for this is <u>multiplication</u>.

### EXAMPLE:

David's <u>three</u> pets live on <u>sprouts</u>.
Each animal needs to be fed <u>10</u>
sprouts a week. How many sprouts
should he buy during his weekly
shopping trip to feed them all?

Oscar

Bruno

Daisy

<u>ANSWER</u>: It's easy. We need 10 sprouts for Oscar, <u>and</u> 10 for Bruno, <u>and</u> 10 for Daisy.
So it's 10+10+10 = 30 sprouts

<u>BUT</u>: Suppose instead he had <u>8 pets</u>.
Then he would need:   10+10+10+10+10+10+10+10 = 80 sprouts
Instead of adding 10 again and again like this, we can use <u>multiplication</u> by saying:
"We need <u>8 lots of 10</u> sprouts, which is <u>8 times 10</u>".
So the answer is  8 × 10 = 80 sprouts.

## Order of Multiplication Doesn't Matter

You could count the number of "false teeth with eyes" toys by saying:

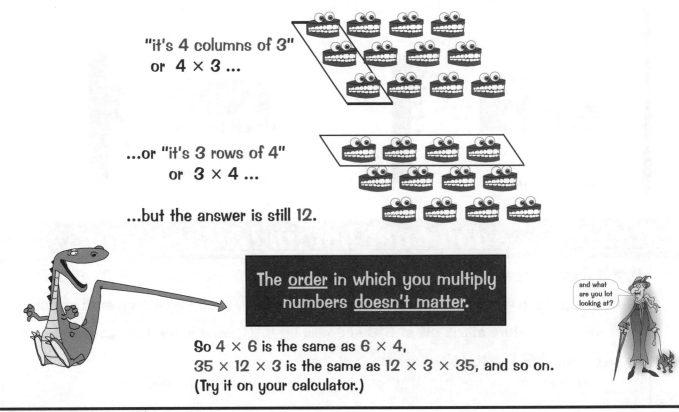

"it's 4 columns of 3"
or  4 × 3 ...

...or "it's 3 rows of 4"
or  3 × 4 ...

...but the answer is still 12.

The <u>order</u> in which you multiply
numbers <u>doesn't matter</u>.

and what
are you lot
looking at?

So 4 × 6 is the same as 6 × 4,
35 × 12 × 3 is the same as 12 × 3 × 35, and so on.
(Try it on your calculator.)

# Multiplication Without a Calculator

## You Need to Know Your Times Tables

The first thing you've got to have sussed is your times tables.
You know what I mean —

"2 times 9 is 18,  3 times 9 is 27, 4 times 9 is 36"...and so on.

Yes, it's boring, but they have to be learnt.
Make sure you know all of them up to "10 times 10 is 100".

*1 times 1 is 1,
2 times 1 is.....
is.....errr.....*

## Multiplication Without a Calculator

## Multiplying by a Single Digit Number

1) Multiply the single digit number by each digit of the big number in turn.

2) Start with Units, then Tens, then Hundreds, ....

3) Each time you get an answer of 10 or more, carry the left digit of the answer to the next column (like you do when you're adding).

**EXAMPLE:** Work out 167 × 4 without using a calculator.

```
  H T U              H T U              H T U              H T U
  1 6 7   7×4=28     1 6 7   6×4=24     1 6 7   1×4=4      1 6 7
×     4            ×     4            ×     4            ×     4
─────────          ─────────          ─────────          ─────────
        8                6 8                6 8              6 6 8
        2              2 2                2 2                2 2
```

So put 8 in the U column...

...carry 2 to the T column.

There was already a 2 under the T column, so put 4+2=6 in it...

...carry 2 to the H column.

There's a carried 2 in the H column, so add it to the 4 to get 6 in the H column

**EXAMPLE:** Work out 931 × 5 without using a calculator.

```
  H T U              H T U              H T U            ThH T U
  9 3 1   1×5=5      9 3 1   3×5=15     9 3 1   9×5=45     9 3 1
×     5            ×     5            ×     5            ×     5
─────────          ─────────          ─────────          ─────────
        5                5 5                5 5            4 6 5 5
                       1                  1                  1
```

So put 5 in the T column...

...carry 1 to the H column.

So 6 goes in the H column (5 plus the carried 1).

Carried 4 goes here because the Thousands column was empty.

# Multiplication Without a Calculator

## Long Multiplication

This needs a lot of practice, but it's okay once you get the hang of it.

**EXAMPLE:** What is 46×14?

This time it looks trickier because you don't have a single-digit number like 4.

> But all you need to do is work out 46×4 and 46 × 10 <u>SEPARATELY</u> and then <u>ADD THEM UP</u>.

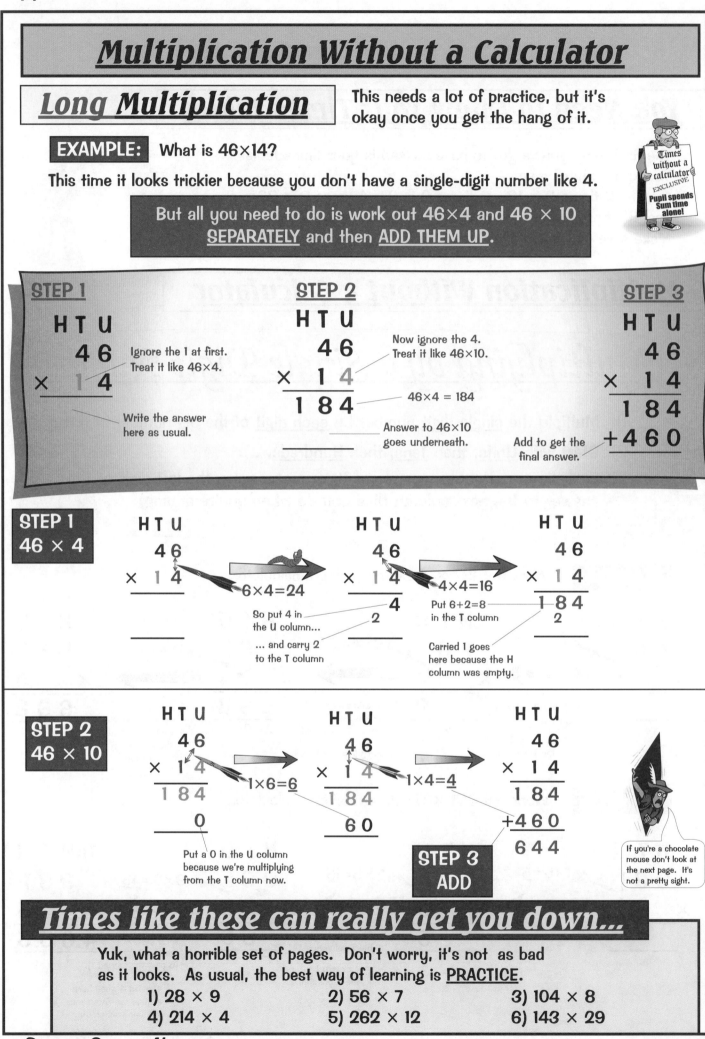

**STEP 1**

```
H T U
  4 6
× 1 4
```

Ignore the 1 at first. Treat it like 46×4.

Write the answer here as usual.

**STEP 2**

```
H T U
    4 6
×   1 4
  1 8 4
```

Now ignore the 4. Treat it like 46×10.

46×4 = 184

Answer to 46×10 goes underneath.

**STEP 3**

```
H T U
    4 6
×   1 4
  1 8 4
+ 4 6 0
```

Add to get the final answer.

---

**STEP 1**
**46 × 4**

```
H T U
  4 6
× 1 4
```
6×4=24

So put 4 in the U column...
... and carry 2 to the T column

```
H T U
  4 6
× 1 4
    4
  2
```

4×4=16

Put 6+2=8 in the T column

Carried 1 goes here because the H column was empty.

```
H T U
  4 6
× 1 4
1 8 4
  2
```

---

**STEP 2**
**46 × 10**

```
H T U
  4 6
× 1 4
1 8 4
  0
```
1×6=6

Put a 0 in the U column because we're multiplying from the T column now.

```
H T U
  4 6
× 1 4
1 8 4
  6 0
```
1×4=4

```
H T U
    4 6
×   1 4
  1 8 4
+ 4 6 0
  6 4 4
```

**STEP 3**
**ADD**

If you're a chocolate mouse don't look at the next page. It's not a pretty sight.

---

## Times like these can really get you down...

Yuk, what a horrible set of pages. Don't worry, it's not as bad as it looks. As usual, the best way of learning is <u>PRACTICE</u>.

1) 28 × 9      2) 56 × 7      3) 104 × 8

4) 214 × 4      5) 262 × 12      6) 143 × 29

# Division

## Division is just Sharing

**EXAMPLE:**

Peter has bought a jar of 20 delicious chocolate mice for his cats. The 4 cats share the mice equally between themselves. The number of mice that each cat gets is "20 shared by 4" which is 5. In maths, they'd call this division or dividing – it sounds more impressive. But it's just sharing.

In symbols:

$$20 \div 4 = 5$$

"divided by"

You might also say "4 into 20 goes 5 times". This means the same thing too. When you're working it out, you'd write it in this form:

$$4\overline{)20}^{\,5}$$

The answer is written on top.

Look — the numbers are the other way round. Put the bigger number inside.

"into...goes"

15 "divided by" **3**,
15 "shared by" **3**,
3 "into" 15 goes...

...all mean the SAME THING

## The Remainder is the Bit Left Over

Suppose the jar had 23 mice instead of 20. When they're shared out, each cat will still get 5, but there'll be 3 left over. We call the bit left over the remainder.

What remainder was that then?

**EXAMPLES:**

1)  6 into 20 goes 3 times with remainder 2   (because 6×3=18)

2)  9 into 57 goes 6 times with remainder 3   (because 9×6=54)

3)  73 ÷ 4 = 18 rem 1   (because 4×18=72)

# Division Without a Calculator

## Times and Divide are Opposites

So if you <u>multiply</u> by some amount then <u>divide</u> by the same amount, you're back where you started.

e.g. $46 \times 3 = 138$, $138 \div 3 = 46$ That's all there is to it.

## Calculations with Divide

You've a choice of two methods for this — <u>Short Division</u> or <u>Long Division</u>. Cool names don't you think? They're pretty much the same, but one needs a bit more ink.

You don't need to remember both methods, just choose the one which works best for you and learn it.

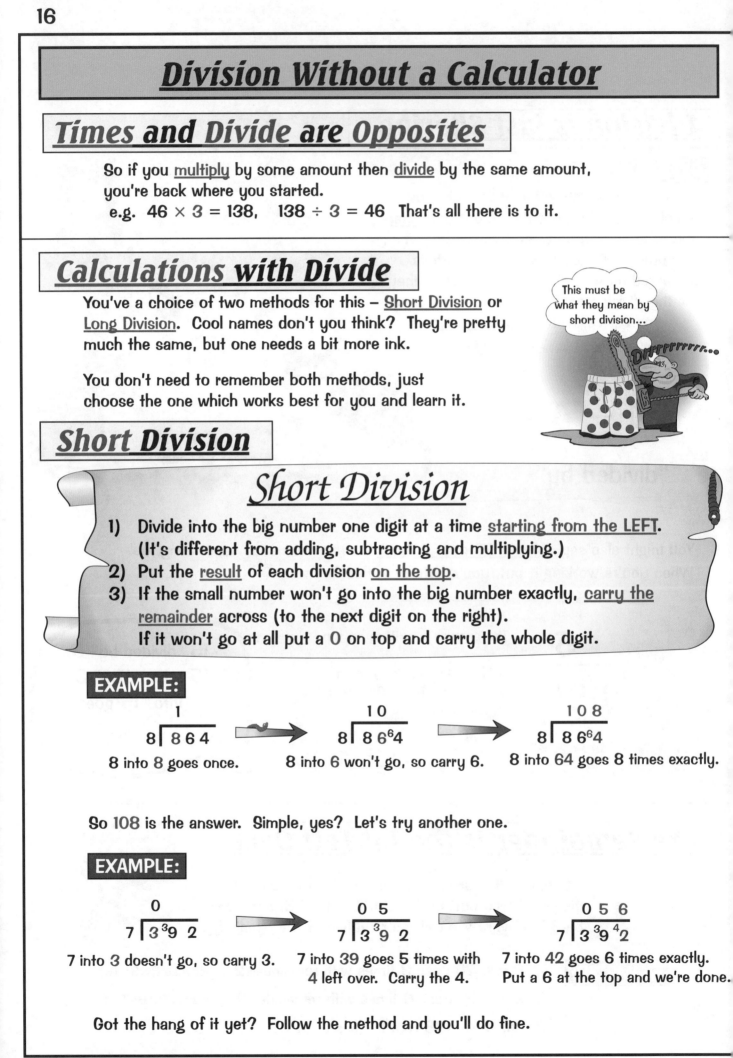

This must be what they mean by short division...

Drrrrppppprrrrr...

## Short Division

### Short Division

1) Divide into the big number one digit at a time <u>starting from the LEFT</u>. (It's different from adding, subtracting and multiplying.)
2) Put the <u>result</u> of each division <u>on the top</u>.
3) If the small number won't go into the big number exactly, <u>carry the remainder</u> across (to the next digit on the right).
   If it won't go at all put a 0 on top and carry the whole digit.

**EXAMPLE:**

$$\begin{array}{r} 1\phantom{00} \\ 8\overline{)8\,6\,4} \end{array}$$

8 into 8 goes once.

$$\begin{array}{r} 1\,0\phantom{0} \\ 8\overline{)8\,6^6\,4} \end{array}$$

8 into 6 won't go, so carry 6.

$$\begin{array}{r} 1\,0\,8 \\ 8\overline{)8\,6^6\,4} \end{array}$$

8 into 64 goes 8 times exactly.

So 108 is the answer. Simple, yes? Let's try another one.

**EXAMPLE:**

$$\begin{array}{r} 0\phantom{00} \\ 7\overline{)3\,^3\!9\,2} \end{array}$$

7 into 3 doesn't go, so carry 3.

$$\begin{array}{r} 0\,5\phantom{0} \\ 7\overline{)3\,^3\!9\,2} \end{array}$$

7 into 39 goes 5 times with 4 left over. Carry the 4.

$$\begin{array}{r} 0\,5\,6 \\ 7\overline{)3\,^3\!9\,^4\!2} \end{array}$$

7 into 42 goes 6 times exactly. Put a 6 at the top and we're done.

Got the hang of it yet? Follow the method and you'll do fine.

# Division Without a Calculator

Okay it looks horrible, I admit. But honestly it's not that bad. Try the questions at the bottom of the next page, and just <u>keep practising</u>.

## Long Division

**EXAMPLE:** Find 2752 ÷ 13 without using a calculator.

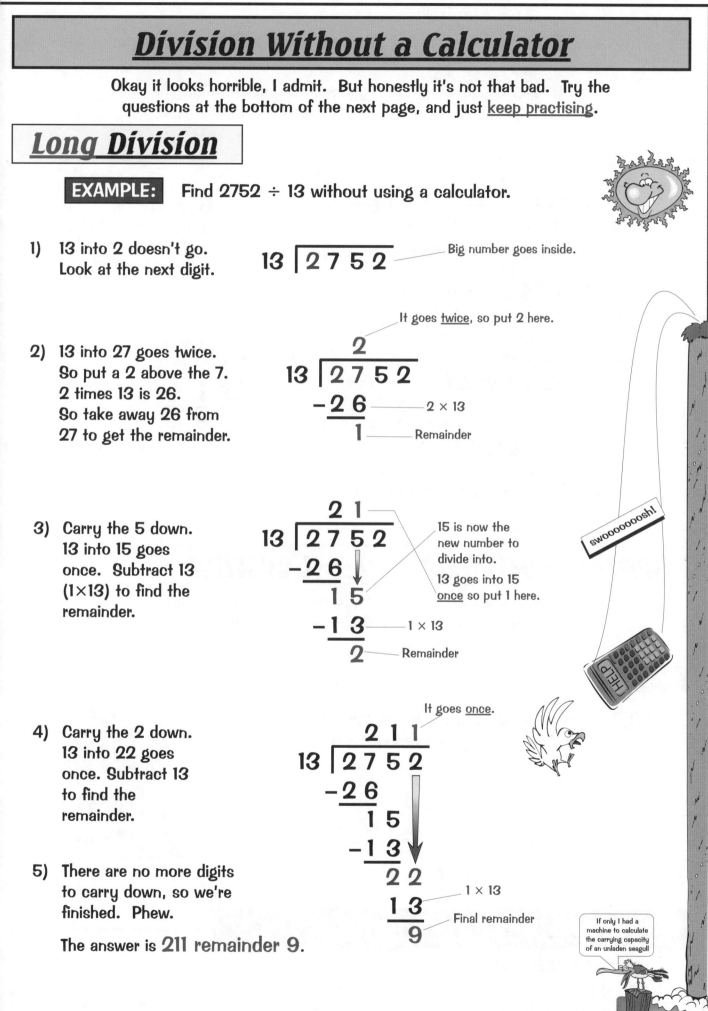

1) 13 into 2 doesn't go. Look at the next digit.

13 ⟌ 2 7 5 2 — Big number goes inside.

2) 13 into 27 goes twice. So put a 2 above the 7. 2 times 13 is 26. So take away 26 from 27 to get the remainder.

It goes <u>twice</u>, so put 2 here.

```
        2
13 | 2 7 5 2
   - 2 6      ── 2 × 13
       1      ── Remainder
```

3) Carry the 5 down. 13 into 15 goes once. Subtract 13 (1×13) to find the remainder.

```
        2 1
13 | 2 7 5 2
   - 2 6  ↓
       1 5
     - 1 3    ── 1 × 13
         2    ── Remainder
```

15 is now the new number to divide into.
13 goes into 15 <u>once</u> so put 1 here.

4) Carry the 2 down. 13 into 22 goes once. Subtract 13 to find the remainder.

It goes <u>once</u>.

```
        2 1 1
13 | 2 7 5 2
   - 2 6
       1 5
     - 1 3  ↓
         2 2
         1 3    ── 1 × 13
           9    ── Final remainder
```

5) There are no more digits to carry down, so we're finished. Phew.

The answer is **211 remainder 9**.

swoooooooosh!

HELP

If only I had a machine to calculate the carrying capacity of an unladen seagull

# Division Without a Calculator

It looks complicated, but if you read carefully through the
example you'll see that it just follows these basic steps:

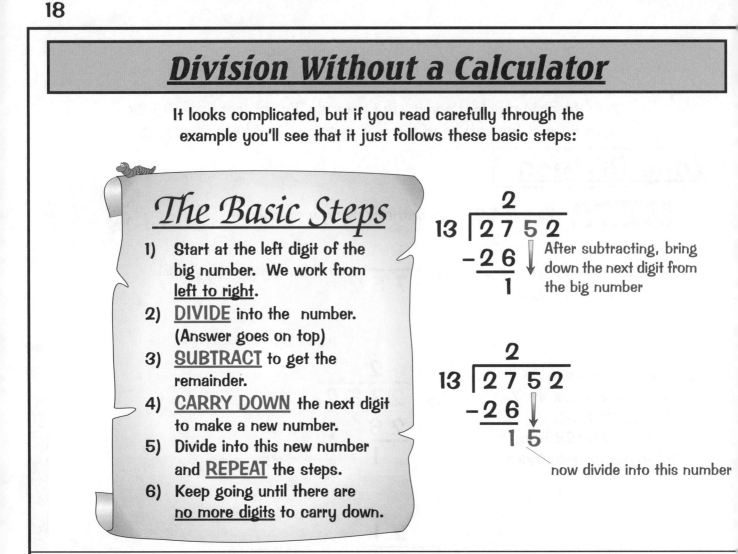

## The Basic Steps

1) Start at the left digit of the
big number. We work from
<u>left to right</u>.
2) <u>DIVIDE</u> into the number.
(Answer goes on top)
3) <u>SUBTRACT</u> to get the
remainder.
4) <u>CARRY DOWN</u> the next digit
to make a new number.
5) Divide into this new number
and <u>REPEAT</u> the steps.
6) Keep going until there are
<u>no more digits</u> to carry down.

After subtracting, bring
down the next digit from
the big number

now divide into this number

# Another Useful Method — Guessing

Sometimes if it's not a hard question, you can just work it
out by guessing and using multiplication to check:

**EXAMPLE:** Work out 104 ÷ 4

**ANSWER:** Since times and divide are opposites,
the "answer <u>times</u> 4" must be 104

| Try 20: | 20 × 4 = 80 | — Too small |
| Try 30: | 30 × 4 = 120 | — Too big |
| Try 25: | 25 × 4 = 100 | — Too small |
| Try 26: | 26 × 4 = 104 | — Spot on |

So 104 ÷ 4 = 26

GUESS WHO?

# Divide, and Conquer those Tests

Try these <u>without</u> a calculator:

1) 242 ÷ 2          2) 84 ÷ 7          3) 370 ÷ 5
4) 134 ÷ 10        5) 216 ÷ 9          6) 5132 ÷ 2

# Typical Questions

Often, you won't simply be given some numbers and told to multiply or add them. Usually you'll be given an <u>exciting real-life</u> situation, which you have to recognise as an adding, subtracting, multiplying or dividing problem.

## A Typical Example

A Sticker Album of the famous boy band "YTS" costs 80p.  Each pack of 20 stickers costs 15p.

1) Chris buys a sticker album and a pack of stickers.
   If he started with a pound, how much does he have now?
   <u>ANSWER:</u>   Easy — just <u>take away</u> the cost of the album and the stickers.
   $$100 - 80 - 15 = 5p$$

2) Lucy buys 6 packs of stickers.  How many stickers has she bought?
   <u>ANSWER:</u>   6 packs with 20 stickers in each.
   So that's 6 lots of 20.  Sounds like <u>multiplication</u> to me.
   $$6 \times 20 = 120 \text{ stickers.}$$

## Some Questions Need a Whole Number Answer

Real-life division questions can be a bit tricky, because they sometimes need a whole number answer.

**EXAMPLE:**  Giant worms cost 20p for a bag of 3.

1) Herman has 72p.  How many bags of worms can he afford?
   <u>ANSWER:</u>   Erm... well we need to know how many 20p's we can get out of 72p.
   So it's how many times 20 goes into 72.  $72 \div 20 = 3$ remainder 12.
   You can't buy bits of a bag, so we can ignore the remainder.
   Herman can buy 3 bags.

2) Stella needs 17 worms to make a cake.  How many bags should she buy?
   <u>ANSWER:</u>   We need to know how many lots of 3 worms make up 17 worms.
   $17 \div 3 = 5$ remainder 2.
   If Stella buys 5 bags of worms, she will only get $5 \times 3 = 15$ worms, which isn't enough.  So to get 17 worms, she needs to buy 6 bags.

## Use Opposites When Checking

It's a good idea to check your answer.  You just do the <u>opposite</u> thing to your answer to check that it gives you back the number <u>you started with</u>.  Remember:

**<u>PLUS</u> and <u>MINUS</u> are <u>OPPOSITES</u>, and so are <u>TIMES</u> and <u>DIVIDE</u>.**

**EXAMPLE:**  What is $342 \div 18$?   Step 1) <u>DO IT:</u>   $342 \div 18 = 19$
Step 2) <u>CHECK IT:</u>   $19 \times 18 = 342$

# Typical Questions

## More Examples...

**EXAMPLE 1:** Write in the missing digit: ☐ 4 × 8 = 272

**ANSWER:** STEP 1) 8 is close to 10, and 272 is close to 300

So if they were the numbers the answer would be 30.

3 0 × 10 = 300

> MAKE A CLEVER GUESS BY WORKING OUT AN EASIER SUM

STEP 2) The answer is close to 30. So try 34:
34 × 8 = <u>272</u>. Great – got it first time.
So the missing digit is **3**

**EXAMPLE 2:** Find the missing number **614.4 ÷ ☐ = 25.6**

> You can use your calculator for this one

### A VERY USEFUL FACT ABOUT DIVIDING TO REMEMBER:
When dividing, the <u>smaller number</u> and the <u>answer</u> can be <u>swapped around</u>.

e.g. **20 ÷ 5 = 4** ⟶ **20 ÷ 4 = 5**

Bigger number    Smaller number    Answer

So using the "Very Useful Fact", we know that 614.4 ÷ 25.6 = ☐
Using your calculator, 614.4 ÷ 25.6 = 24    So 24 is the missing number.

# Brackets _Show You Which Bit_ of a Sum to Do First

Trickier calculations involve <u>more than one</u> operation — e.g. <u>add</u> and <u>times</u>.
To make sure you do them in the <u>right order</u>, use this important rule:

### ALWAYS DO THE BIT IN BRACKETS FIRST

**EXAMPLE:** Work out (12 + 6) × 4:

Step 1) <u>WORK OUT THE BRACKETS</u>    (12 + 6) = 18

Step 2) <u>DO THE MULTIPLICATION</u>    So now you've got...    18 × 4 = 72

# Decimals

Decimals are really useful if you want to say "between 7 and 8" but need to know <u>where</u> in between. Is it a little bit more than 7? More or less in the middle? Just below 8?

## So What are These Decimals...

It's like you did on page 1, but smaller!
Just as you have Units, Tens, Hundreds and so on, you have <u>Tenths</u> and <u>Hundreths</u>, going in the other direction. To stop them getting mixed up we use a dot (but everyone calls it a <u>decimal point</u>, to sound clever).

| Tens | Units | . | Tenths |
|------|-------|---|--------|
| 3 | 2 | . | 1 |
| 3 | 2 | . | 9 |
| 3 | 2 | . | 5 |

is just a bit bigger than 32

is almost 33

is right in the middle

We can see where decimals are by looking at the number line:

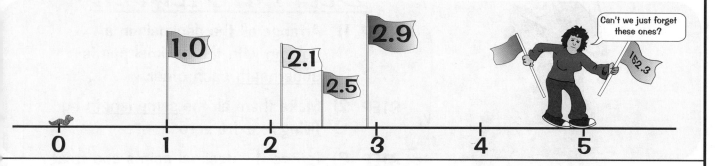

## Adding and Subtracting Decimals is Easy

I know. It's easy for <u>me</u> to say they're not hard — I don't have to do your Tests. But if you can add and subtract normal (whole) numbers, it's simple.

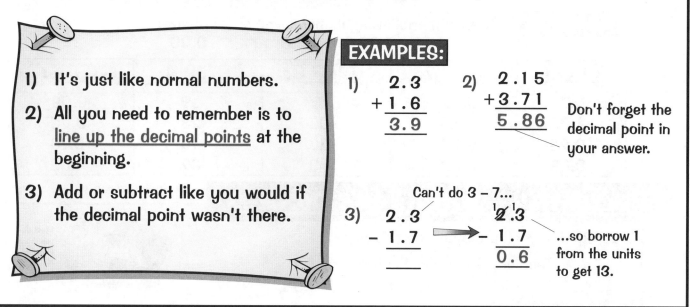

1) It's just like normal numbers.

2) All you need to remember is to <u>line up the decimal points</u> at the beginning.

3) Add or subtract like you would if the decimal point wasn't there.

EXAMPLES:

1)
```
  2.3
+ 1.6
-----
  3.9
```

2)
```
  2.15
+ 3.71
------
  5.86
```
Don't forget the decimal point in your answer.

Can't do 3 – 7...

3)
```
  2.3
- 1.7
-----
```
→
```
  ¹2.¹3
- 1.7
------
  0.6
```
...so borrow 1 from the units to get 13.

# Decimals

In your Tests you'll have to be able to <u>arrange</u> a list of decimal numbers in order of <u>size</u>.

## Ordering Decimals *Like Whole Numbers*

This is easy when you place the numbers <u>underneath</u> each other and <u>line up</u> the decimal points.

| It's easy to see that | 0.30 |
| is more than | 0.07 |

Unfortunately things can get a bit trickier, especially if there are a lot of numbers and they aren't written tidily <u>underneath one another</u>.

| Just as | 30 |
| is more than | 7 |

So when in doubt, go for:

## The *Foolproof* Method of *Ordering Decimals*

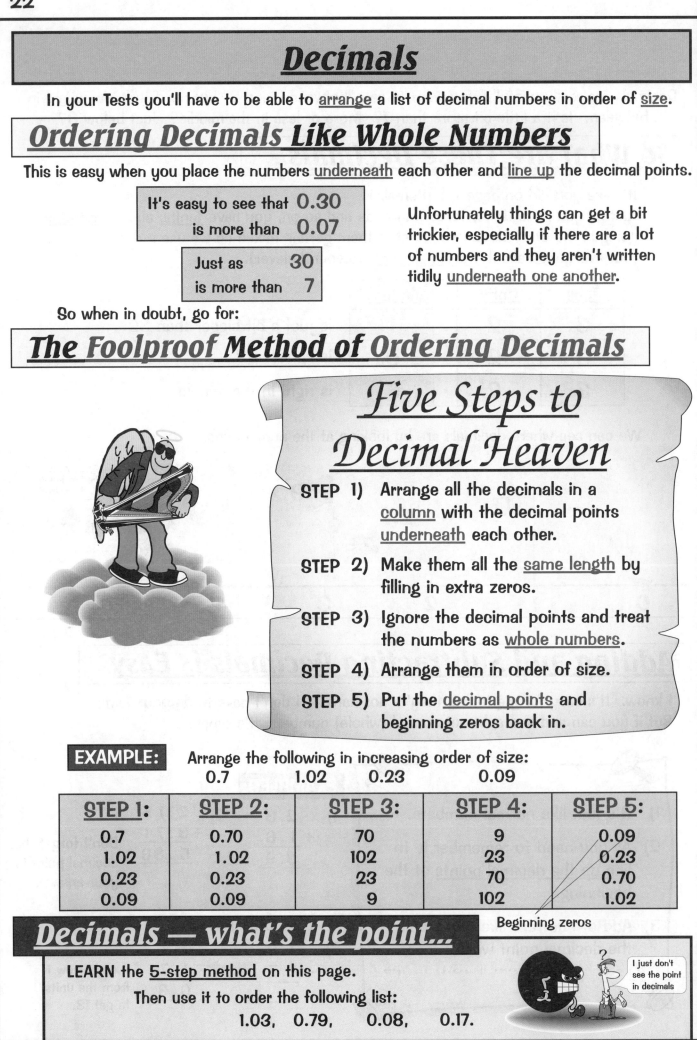

# *Five Steps to Decimal Heaven*

**STEP 1)** Arrange all the decimals in a <u>column</u> with the decimal points <u>underneath</u> each other.

**STEP 2)** Make them all the <u>same length</u> by filling in extra zeros.

**STEP 3)** Ignore the decimal points and treat the numbers as <u>whole numbers</u>.

**STEP 4)** Arrange them in order of size.

**STEP 5)** Put the <u>decimal points</u> and beginning zeros back in.

**EXAMPLE:** Arrange the following in increasing order of size:

0.7        1.02        0.23        0.09

| STEP 1: | STEP 2: | STEP 3: | STEP 4: | STEP 5: |
|---------|---------|---------|---------|---------|
| 0.7 | 0.70 | 70 | 9 | 0.09 |
| 1.02 | 1.02 | 102 | 23 | 0.23 |
| 0.23 | 0.23 | 23 | 70 | 0.70 |
| 0.09 | 0.09 | 9 | 102 | 1.02 |

Beginning zeros

## *Decimals — what's the point...*

**LEARN** the <u>5-step method</u> on this page.

Then use it to order the following list:

1.03,    0.79,    0.08,    0.17.

I just don't see the point in decimals

# Rounding Off

## Rounding Off Numbers

There are four easy ways they might ask you to round off a number:
1) To the nearest TEN.
2) To the nearest HUNDRED.
3) To the nearest THOUSAND.
4) To the nearest WHOLE NUMBER.

This isn't difficult so long as you remember the 2 RULES:

## The Two Rounding Rules

1) The number always lies between two possible answers, just choose the one it's nearest to.

2) If the number is exactly in the middle, then round it up.

**EXAMPLE:**

On average, a superhero will accidentally fly into 1851 windows during his professional career. How many is 1851 to the nearest thousand?

ANSWER:   1851 is between 1000 and 2000, but it is nearer to 2000.

**EXAMPLE:**   Last year, there were 15 recorded cases of "superhero turns into a computer" syndrome. How many is 15 to the nearest ten?

ANSWER:   15 is exactly in the middle of 10 and 20, so round it up to 20.

**EXAMPLE:**

Flying superheroes need to eat lots of baked beans to enhance their super powers. Their recommended daily allowance is 13.8 kilograms. What is 13.8 to the nearest whole number?

ANSWER:   13.8 is between 13 and 14 but it is closer to 14.

# Rounding Off

When you have <u>DECIMAL NUMBERS</u> you might have to round them off to the nearest whole number. The trouble is, they could also ask you to round them off to <u>ONE DECIMAL PLACE</u> (or possibly <u>TWO decimal places</u>). This isn't too bad but you do have to learn some rules for it:

## Rounding Off to Decimal Places

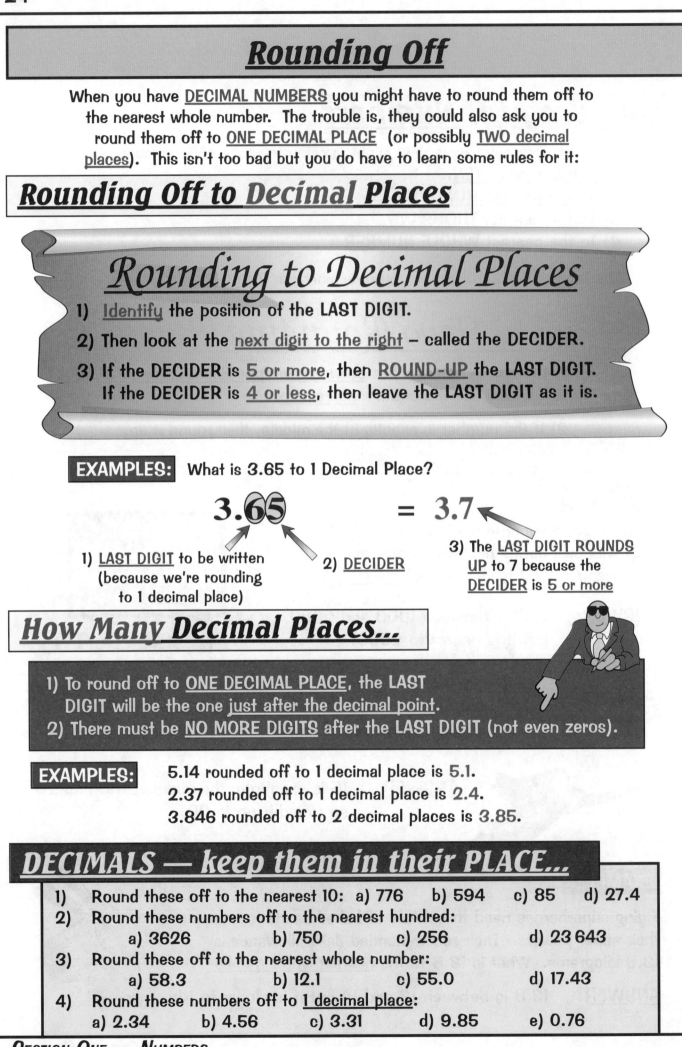

### Rounding to Decimal Places

1) <u>Identify</u> the position of the LAST DIGIT.

2) Then look at the <u>next digit to the right</u> – called the DECIDER.

3) If the DECIDER is <u>5 or more</u>, then <u>ROUND-UP</u> the LAST DIGIT.
   If the DECIDER is <u>4 or less</u>, then leave the LAST DIGIT as it is.

**EXAMPLES:** What is 3.65 to 1 Decimal Place?

$$3.65 \qquad = \quad 3.7$$

1) <u>LAST DIGIT</u> to be written (because we're rounding to 1 decimal place)

2) <u>DECIDER</u>

3) The <u>LAST DIGIT ROUNDS UP</u> to 7 because the <u>DECIDER</u> is <u>5 or more</u>

## How Many Decimal Places...

1) To round off to <u>ONE DECIMAL PLACE</u>, the LAST DIGIT will be the one <u>just after the decimal point</u>.

2) There must be <u>NO MORE DIGITS</u> after the LAST DIGIT (not even zeros).

**EXAMPLES:**
5.14 rounded off to 1 decimal place is 5.1.
2.37 rounded off to 1 decimal place is 2.4.
3.846 rounded off to 2 decimal places is 3.85.

## DECIMALS — keep them in their PLACE...

1) Round these off to the nearest 10:  a) 776  b) 594  c) 85  d) 27.4

2) Round these numbers off to the nearest hundred:
   a) 3626  b) 750  c) 256  d) 23 643

3) Round these off to the nearest whole number:
   a) 58.3  b) 12.1  c) 55.0  d) 17.43

4) Round these numbers off to <u>1 decimal place</u>:
   a) 2.34  b) 4.56  c) 3.31  d) 9.85  e) 0.76

# *Mental Arithmetic*

You really need to get the hang of this mental arithmetic lark. It will save you loads of time in the Test if you get it sorted now.

## *TO MULTIPLY ANY NUMBER BY 10*

Keep the decimal point where it is and move the digits <u>ONE PLACE</u> to the <u>LEFT</u> and add a zero if needed.

**EXAMPLES:**

Think of this as 35.0

$35 \times 10 = 35.0 \times 10 = 3 5 0$

$162 \times 10 = 162.0 \times 10 = 1 6 2 0$

$8.625 \times 10 = 8 6 . 2 5$

## *TO MULTIPLY ANY NUMBER BY 100*

Keep the decimal point where it is and move the digits <u>TWO PLACES</u> to the <u>LEFT</u> and add zeros if needed.

**EXAMPLES:**

$618 \times 100 = 618.00 \times 100 = 6 1 8 0 0$

$75.9 \times 100 = 75.90 \times 100 = 7 5 9 0$

$12.573 \times 100 = 1 2 5 7 . 3$

## *TO MULTIPLY ANY NUMBER BY 1000*

Keep the decimal point where it is and move the digits <u>THREE PLACES</u> to the <u>LEFT</u> and add zeros if needed.

**EXAMPLES:**

$194 \times 1000 = 194.000 \times 1000 = 1 9 4 0 0 0$

$27.11 \times 1000 = 27.110 \times 1000 = 2 7 1 1 0$

$4.3856 \times 1000 = 4 3 8 5 . 6$

## *TO MULTIPLY OR DIVIDE BY NUMBERS LIKE 20, 800, ETC.*

<u>Multiply (or divide) by 2 or 8 etc. FIRST</u>, then move the digits. The number of places you move them depends on <u>how many noughts</u> there are. So you would move the digits 1 place for 20, 2 places for 800 and so on.

**EXAMPLE:** To find $431 \times 200$, first multiply by 2: $431 \times 2 = 862$, then move the digits 2 places to the left = $8 6 2 0 0$

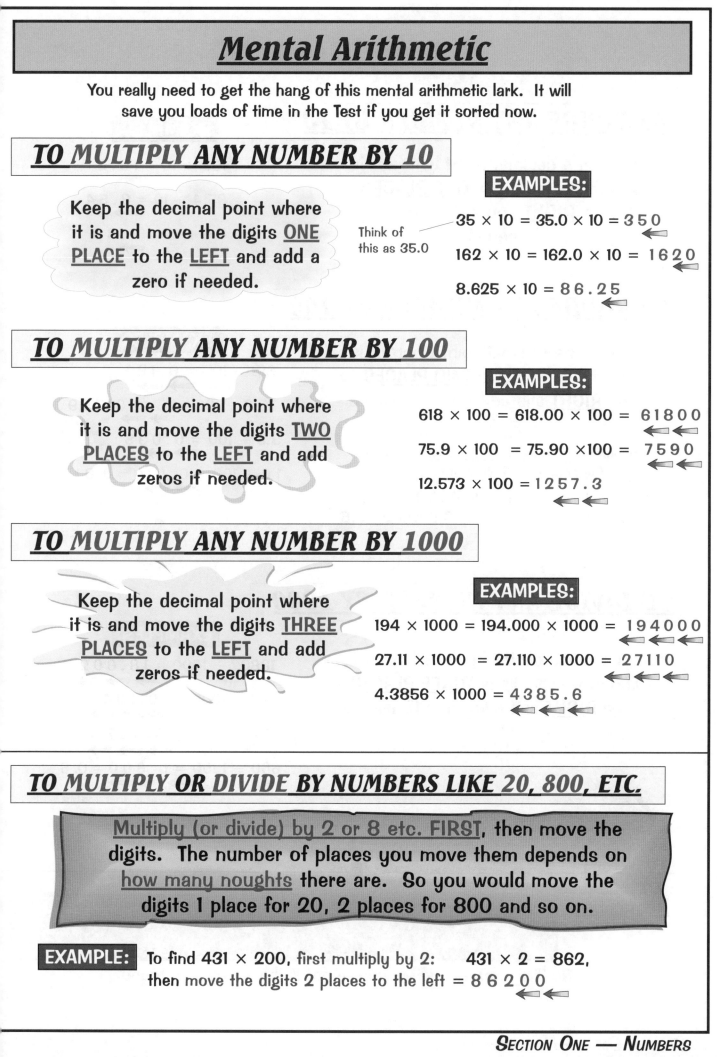

# Mental Arithmetic

## TO DIVIDE ANY NUMBER BY 10

Keep the decimal point where it is and move the digits <u>ONE PLACE</u> to the <u>RIGHT</u> and add zeros if needed.

**EXAMPLES:**

$162 \div 10 = 16.2$

$35.4 \div 10 = 3.54$

$8.6 \div 10 = 0.86$

## TO DIVIDE ANY NUMBER BY 100

Keep the decimal point where it is and move the digits <u>TWO PLACES</u> to the <u>RIGHT</u> and add zeros if needed.

Remember to <u>remove unnecessary</u> zeros at the end, e.g. 13.30 is just 13.3

<u>AND</u> there has to be a digit to the left of the decimal point, so you'd have to put 0.5 instead of .5

**EXAMPLES:**

$618 \div 100 = 6.18$

$75.9 \div 100 = \quad 0.759$

We need to add a zero because there are no more digits to the left of the 3.

$3.5 \div 100 = 0.035$

$1.0 \div 100 = 0.010 = 0.01$

This zero has no effect, so we can remove it.

## TO DIVIDE ANY NUMBER BY 1000

Keep the decimal point where it is and move the digits <u>THREE PLACES</u> to the <u>RIGHT</u> and add zeros if needed.

**EXAMPLES:**

$18602 \div 1000 = 18.602$

$194 \div 1000 = 0.194$

$27.11 \div 1000 = 0.02711$

$600 \div 1000 = 0.600 = 0.6$

These zeros have no effect, so we can remove them.

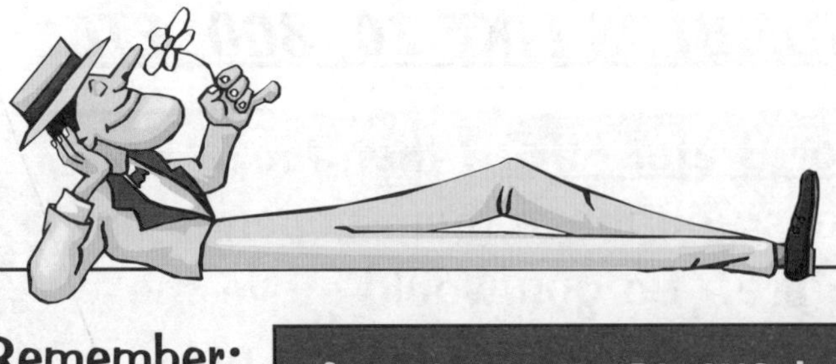

<u>Remember:</u> If you're MULTIPLYING by 10 or 100, the answer will be BIGGER. If you're DIVIDING by 10 or 100, the answer will be SMALLER.

So if it's not, you know you've got it the wrong way round.

# Mental Arithmetic

## Adding and Subtracting in Your Head

It's good to know a few tricks for working things out in your head. They can save you precious time in the Tests.

**EXAMPLE:** Work out 35 – 12 in your head.

**ANSWER:** Just split it up into <u>2 EASY SUMS</u>:
<u>Taking away 12</u> is the same as
<u>taking away 10</u> and <u>then 2</u>.

Even a farmyard animal could do it now.

> 35 take away 10 is 25

> 25 take away 2 is 23

> So 35 – 12 = 23

Mmm... swede!

Boris the whizz-pig

**EXAMPLE:** What's 57 – 9?

**ANSWER:** <u>Taking away 9</u> is the same as <u>taking away 10</u> and then <u>adding 1</u>.
57 minus 10 is 47...  ...47 plus 1 is 48, so the answer's 48.

**EXAMPLE:** What's 646 + 97?

**ANSWER:** This one looks really nasty. But if you do it in two steps, it's a piece of cake. Instead of <u>adding 97</u>, we can <u>add 100</u>, then <u>take away 3</u> (97 = 100 – 3).

"646 plus 100 is 746....

...746 minus 3 is 743...

... So 646 + 97 = 743."

**EXAMPLE:** Work out 3710 – 992 in your head.

**ANSWER:** This looks even harder than the last one, but we can solve it the same way.
Break it up into two parts again, and it's easy:
992 + 8 = 1000, so <u>take away 1000</u> first, then <u>add 8</u>.

"3710 minus 1000 is 2710....

...2710 plus 8 is 2718...

... So 3710 – 992 = 2718."

## Go forth and multiply...

1) Work out:  a) 14 × 100  b) 87.1 × 10  c) 25 × 100  d) 11 × 60
2) Work out:  a) 56 ÷ 10  b) 426 ÷ 100  c) 12.7 ÷ 10  d) 666 ÷ 30
3) Work out the following <u>in your head</u>:
  a) 5 + 13  b) 18 – 15  c) 74 – 22  d) 354 + 9  e) 354 + 99
  f) 28 – 9  g) 143 – 99  h) 34 + 98  i) 3142 + 198  j) 5832 – 497

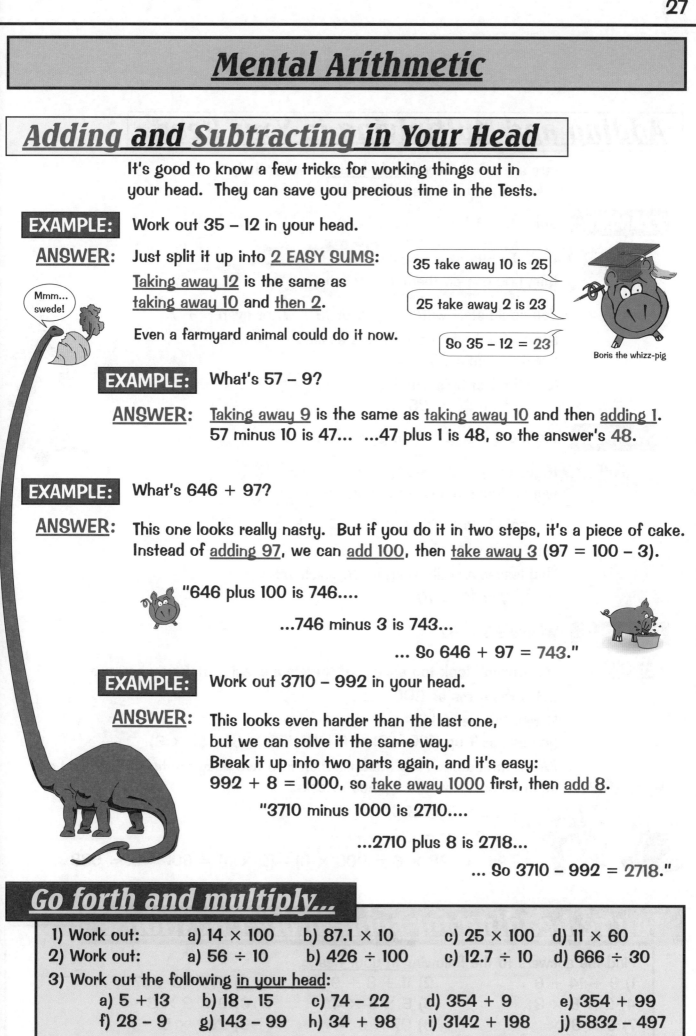

# Mental Arithmetic

## Adding and Multiplying in Your Head

Here are a few more <u>handy tricks</u> that can help make some questions a bit easier to solve.

**EXAMPLE:** Solve 5 + 13 + 7 in your head.

**ANSWER:** If <u>all</u> the bits of a question are additions, then you can do them in any order.

You could start with 5 + 13, or 13 + 7, or even 5 + 7.

Start with the bit you think is easiest.

I reckon that's 13 + 7 = 20

Now the last bit's simple:

5 + 20 = 25

**EXAMPLE:** Work out 7 × 2 × 5 in your head.

**ANSWER:** If you've <u>only</u> got multiplications, you can do them in any order you like, too.

You could start with 7 × 2, or 2 × 5, or 7 × 5.

Let's start with 2 × 5 = 10

That leaves a really easy bit to finish with:

7 × 10 = 70

**EXAMPLE:** What's 98 × 6?

**ANSWER:** This doesn't look too easy, but there's a sneaky trick you can use.

98 is the same as (100 − 2).

Here's the clever bit:
you can split up (100 − 2) × 6 into (100 × 6) − (2 × 6).

We've turned one hard multiplication into two easy multiplications and a subtraction. Now it's a piece of cake.

100 × 6 = 600

2 × 6 = 12

So    98 × 6 = (100 × 6) − (2 × 6) = 600 − 12 = 588

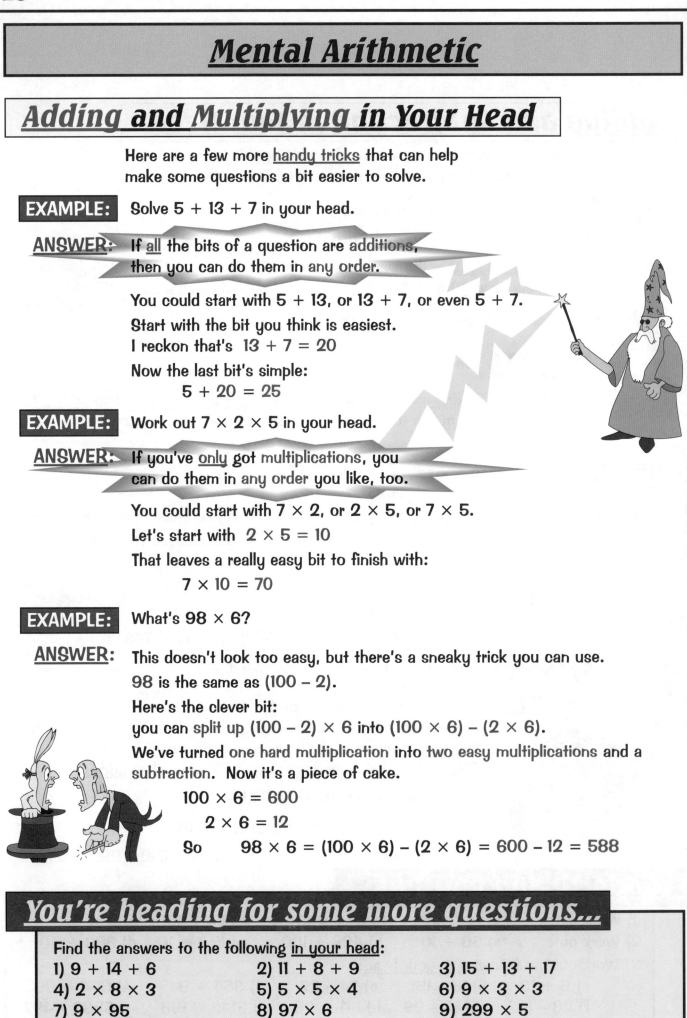

## You're heading for some more questions...

Find the answers to the following <u>in your head</u>:

1) 9 + 14 + 6           2) 11 + 8 + 9           3) 15 + 13 + 17

4) 2 × 8 × 3           5) 5 × 5 × 4           6) 9 × 3 × 3

7) 9 × 95           8) 97 × 6           9) 299 × 5

# Calculations With Money

A favourite type of question they like to ask you in tests is comparing the "value for money" of 2 or 3 similar items. It'll either be a "different number of items" problem, or a "different weights" problem.

## Which Multipack is Better Value?

**EXAMPLE:** The new soft drink Sproutade can be bought in multipacks of 4 cans or 6 cans. The 4-can multipack costs £1.20. The 6-can multipack costs £1.62. The question is: Which of these is "**THE BEST VALUE FOR MONEY**"?

4 cans at £1.20

**ANSWER:**

For each one, work out:
## PRICE ÷ NUMBER OF ITEMS
to find how much one item costs.

6 cans at £1.62

| | |
|---|---|
| 4-PACK: | 120p ÷ 4 = 30p PER CAN |
| 6-PACK: | 162p ÷ 6 = 27p PER CAN |

So the 6-PACK IS BETTER VALUE FOR MONEY because the price of a can from the 6-pack is 3 pence cheaper than a can from the 4-pack.

## Which Weight is Better Value?

**EXAMPLE:**

The local Royalty Cinema sells popcorn in three different sizes, Small, Regular and Large. Which one is the best value for money?

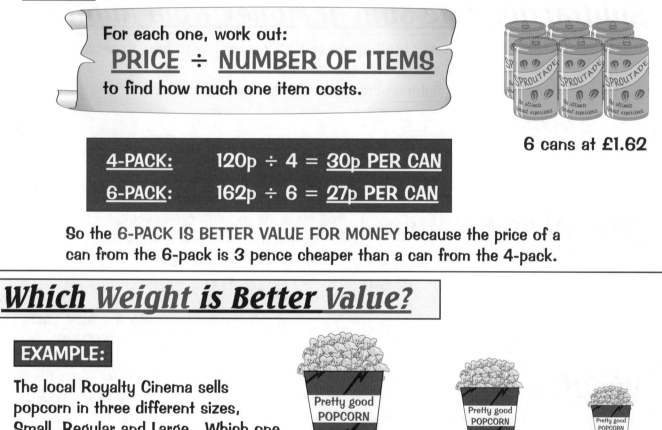

400 g at 180p     250 g at 120p     100 g at 80p

**ANSWER:**

For each one, work out:
## PRICE ÷ WEIGHT
to find how much 1 g of it costs.

| |
|---|
| 180p ÷ 400 = 0.45p per gram |
| 120p ÷ 250 = 0.48p per gram |
| 80p ÷ 100 = 0.80p per gram |

So we can now see that the 400 g box is the best value for money because it's the cheapest per gram.

# Calculations With Money

Money sums are easy. They're just like normal number sums — all you need to remember is to put the decimal points and pound signs in the right place.

## Adding Two Sums of Money

*If you're not sure about these then look back at pages 5-18.*

Doris buys a £6.37 fossilised cucumber and a £9.75 pro-celebrity bog-snorkelling video. How much does she spend altogether?

1) Add the pence.
```
  £6.37
+ £9.75
  £    2
       1
```

2) Add the tens.
```
  £6.37
+ £9.75
  £ .12
    1 1
```

3) Add the pounds.
```
  £6.37
+ £9.75
  £16.12
    1 1
```

**Remember to line up the decimal points.**

So she spends £16.12.

## Subtracting One Sum of Money from Another

Sarah has £5.65. Her nasty brother steals £1.99 from her to buy strawberries for his pet snail. How much money has she got left?

1) Subtract the pence.
```
  £5.⁵6̷¹5
− £1.99
       6
```

2) Subtract the tens.
```
  £⁴5̷.¹⁵6̷¹5
− £1.99
      .66
```

3) Subtract the pounds.
```
  £⁴5̷.¹⁵6̷¹5
− £1.99
  £3.66
```

**Line up the decimal points.**

So she has £3.66 left.

## Multiplying Money

Neil buys six mouldy cheesecakes at £4.50 each. What is the total cost?

1) Multiply the pence.
```
  £ 4.50
×     6
      0
```

2) Multiply the tens.
```
  £ 4.50
×     6
    .00
   3
```

3) Multiply the pounds.
```
  £ 4.50
×     6
  £27.00
   3
```

So the total cost is £27.00.

## Dividing Money

The four Fitzgeranium children win £4.76 when their pet racing hamster comes last in the Le Mans Rally. If they share their prize equally between them, how much do they get each?

1) Divide the pounds.
```
   1.
4 ) 4.76
```

2) Divide the tens.
```
   1.1
4 ) 4.7³6
```

3) Divide the pence.
```
   1.19
4 ) 4.7³6
```

**Always begin at the pound end with division.**

So they'll get £1.19 each.

## I can't take MONEY more of these...

1) Froggatt's "Snail 'n' Pea Soup" comes in three different sizes:

The 200g tin at 50p, the 350g tin at 70p and the Farmhouse Size, 650g, at 117p. Work out which one is the best value for money. (And don't just guess!)

2) Work out the following:  a) £4.92 + £2.65    b) £20.50 − £4.05
   c) £6.99 × 3    d) £18.30 ÷ 6

# _Practice Questions_

Try the following questions without using your calculator, unless it says that you can.

1) Write eighty-seven thousand, nine hundred and seventy-four as a number.

2) Order the following list: 252, 723, 265 , 997, 253.

3) Order the following list: 352, 142, 635, 2854, 12, 53, 11 452, 153.

4) Work out   a) 23 + 71       b) 835 + 273       c) 142 + 969

5) Work out   a) 26 – 17       b) 75 – 28       c) 942 – 269

6) Work out   a) 5 × 243       b) 2 × 754       c) 42 × 46

7) Work out   a) 48 ÷ 7       b) 207 ÷ 9       c) 983 ÷ 3
     Give the remainder if necessary.

8) Write in the missing digit:     $\boxed{\phantom{x}}6 \times 7 = 322$

9) Write in the missing three–digit number:    $\boxed{\phantom{xxx}} \div 10 = 30$

10) Find the missing number:       $774 \div \boxed{\phantom{xx}} = 64.5$    You can use your calculator for this one.

11) Work out     a) 35.13 + 76.32      b) 17.3 – 16.7

12) Order the following numbers:   23.3    23.1    23.11    37.6    37.06

13) Round off 6447.85 to     a) the nearest thousand    b) 1 decimal place
                             c) the nearest ten          d) the nearest whole number

14) Find 3.5 × 100.

15) What's      a) 12 ÷ 100     b) 40 ÷ 200?

16) Work out      a) 14 + 11     b) 65 + 13   in your head.

17) Work out      a) 84 – 9      b) 375 + 98        c) 194 × 4

You can use me for questions 18 and 19, you lucky thing.

18)    A single can of cola costs 37p.      A multipack of 6 cans costs £2.10.

     Which is better value for money?

19) The local video store sells Chocolate Sludge ice cream in 3 different sizes of tubs.

     200 ml for £1.15      500 ml for £3.80      1000 ml for £5.45

     Which is the best value for money?

20) Simon ate 12 mustard and vinegar sandwiches. Each sandwich cost 89p.
     Work out the total cost of the 12 sandwiches.
     Write the answer   a) in pence,   b) in pounds.

21) David wants a stretchy alien toy which costs £2.99. Becky wants a glow in the dark
     yo-yo costing £1.50. How much will it cost their mother to buy these items?

# Calculators

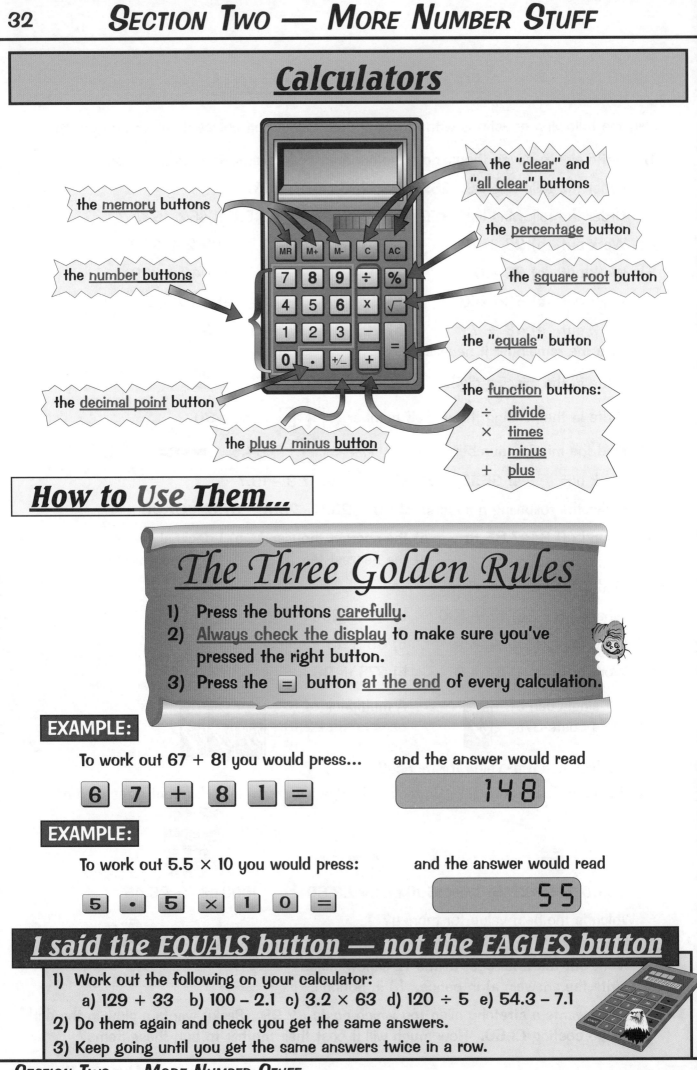

the memory buttons

the number buttons

the decimal point button

the plus / minus button

the "clear" and "all clear" buttons

the percentage button

the square root button

the "equals" button

the function buttons:
÷ divide
× times
− minus
+ plus

## How to Use Them...

# The Three Golden Rules

1) Press the buttons carefully.
2) Always check the display to make sure you've pressed the right button.
3) Press the ☐ button at the end of every calculation.

**EXAMPLE:**

To work out 67 + 81 you would press...

6 7 + 8 1 =

and the answer would read

148

**EXAMPLE:**

To work out 5.5 × 10 you would press:

5 • 5 × 1 0 =

and the answer would read

55

## I said the EQUALS button — not the EAGLES button

1) Work out the following on your calculator:
   a) 129 + 33  b) 100 − 2.1  c) 3.2 × 63  d) 120 ÷ 5  e) 54.3 − 7.1
2) Do them again and check you get the same answers.
3) Keep going until you get the same answers twice in a row.

# Fractions

Remember decimals?  Well, fractions are another way
to show numbers that are <u>in between</u> whole numbers.

When something is divided up into <u>equal bits</u>, that's where fractions come in.

## There are *Two Bits to Every Fraction*

### NUMERATOR
This tells you how many
bits <u>we're talking about</u>.

### DENOMINATOR
This is how many bits
<u>there are altogether</u>.

$$\frac{3}{4}$$

To <u>compare</u> a <u>DECIMAL</u> and a
fraction, just stick the fraction
into your <u>calculator</u> — by
dividing the top by the bottom.

You always read the <u>numerator</u> as a <u>normal number</u> ("one", "two", "three" etc).

The <u>denominator</u> is a bit more sneaky, because there are <u>3 special cases</u>:

For $\frac{1}{2}$ you would say "<u>one half</u>",
for $\frac{1}{3}$ you'd say "<u>one third</u>"
and for $\frac{1}{4}$ you would say "<u>one quarter</u>".

For the others you just add a "<u>ths</u>" sound — fif<u>ths</u>, six<u>ths</u>, seven<u>ths</u>, ...

**EXAMPLE:**  Gemma has made a mistake on question 4 of her maths homework.
Mrs Verystrict says she has to eat <u>8 tins</u> of Ace Roast Beans as punishment.

Gemma manages to eat <u>5 tins</u> before her stomach starts to hurt too much to carry on.
What <u>fraction</u> of the total amount did she eat?  What fraction is left?

<u>ANSWER</u>:   She's eaten 5 of the 8 tins, so it's $\frac{5}{8}$ (we say "five eighths").
There are three tins left.  So it's $\frac{3}{8}$ (we say "three eighths").

Mixed fractions are when you have fractions and whole numbers <u>together</u>.

## Mixed *Fractions*

If you write $1\frac{1}{2}$, it's the same as $1+\frac{1}{2}$... and $5\frac{3}{4}$ is the same as $5+\frac{3}{4}$.

They're said as "<u>one and a half</u>" and "<u>five and three quarters</u>".  That's it.

**EXAMPLE:**

I have $1\frac{1}{2}$ worm-eaten grapefruit.

**EXAMPLE:**

The worm-eating
grapefruit is chasing $5\frac{3}{4}$ worms.

# Fractions

## Divide Top by Bottom to get a Decimal

It's easy to turn fractions into decimals using your calculator. Just <u>divide the top by the bottom</u>.

**EXAMPLE:** Convert $\frac{1}{8}$ to a decimal.

**ANSWER:** <u>Divide 1 by 8:</u>
$1 \div 8 = 0.125$.

To change decimals to fractions you've got to look at where the <u>last digit</u> after the decimal point is.

The last digit is in the thousandths column, so this is written as <u>256 thousandths</u>, or $\frac{256}{1000}$.

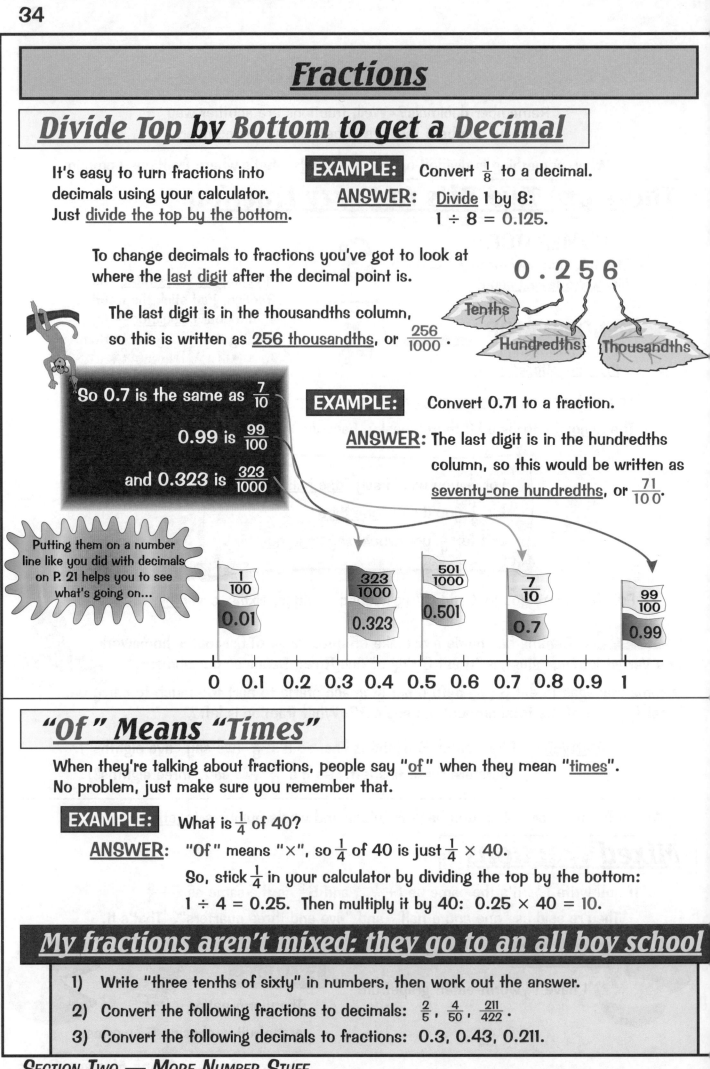

So 0.7 is the same as $\frac{7}{10}$

0.99 is $\frac{99}{100}$

and 0.323 is $\frac{323}{1000}$

**EXAMPLE:** Convert 0.71 to a fraction.

**ANSWER:** The last digit is in the hundredths column, so this would be written as <u>seventy-one hundredths</u>, or $\frac{71}{100}$.

Putting them on a number line like you did with decimals on P. 21 helps you to see what's going on...

## "Of" Means "Times"

When they're talking about fractions, people say "<u>of</u>" when they mean "<u>times</u>". No problem, just make sure you remember that.

**EXAMPLE:** What is $\frac{1}{4}$ of 40?

**ANSWER:** "Of" means "×", so $\frac{1}{4}$ of 40 is just $\frac{1}{4} \times 40$.

So, stick $\frac{1}{4}$ in your calculator by dividing the top by the bottom: $1 \div 4 = 0.25$. Then multiply it by 40: $0.25 \times 40 = 10$.

## My fractions aren't mixed: they go to an all boy school

1) Write "three tenths of sixty" in numbers, then work out the answer.

2) Convert the following fractions to decimals: $\frac{2}{5}$, $\frac{4}{50}$, $\frac{211}{422}$.

3) Convert the following decimals to fractions: 0.3, 0.43, 0.211.

# Fractions

## Fraction Bars

This is an easy way to see how big a fraction is.

**EXAMPLE:** A fraction bar for $\frac{1}{4}$

To do this it helps to choose a good length for your bar. 12 cm is often a good one.

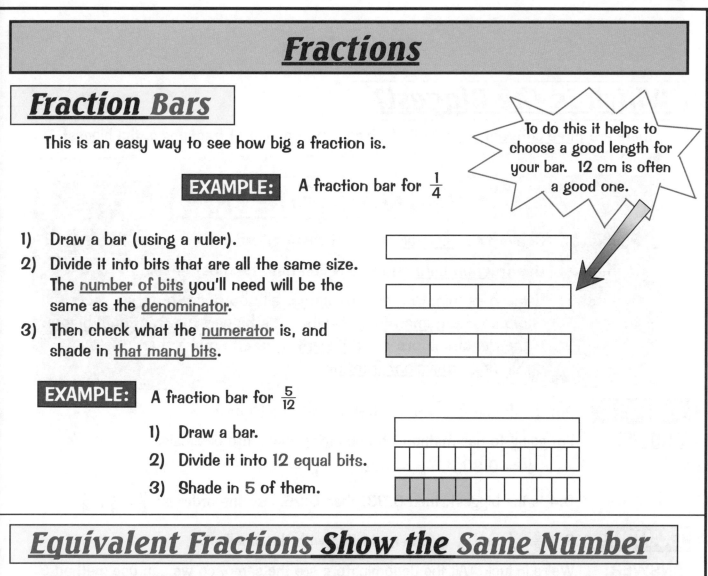

1) Draw a bar (using a ruler).
2) Divide it into bits that are all the same size. The <u>number of bits</u> you'll need will be the same as the <u>denominator</u>.
3) Then check what the <u>numerator</u> is, and shade in <u>that many bits</u>.

**EXAMPLE:** A fraction bar for $\frac{5}{12}$

1) Draw a bar.
2) Divide it into 12 equal bits.
3) Shade in 5 of them.

# Equivalent Fractions Show the Same Number

<u>Equivalent fractions</u> are ones that look <u>different</u> from each other, but are really the <u>same</u>, like $\frac{1}{2}$ and $\frac{2}{4}$. You can make an equivalent fraction by multiplying or dividing the top and bottom by the same number.

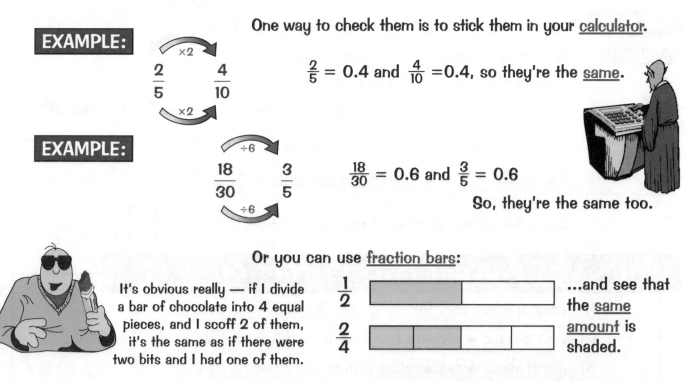

**EXAMPLE:**

$$\frac{2}{5} \xrightarrow{\times 2} \frac{4}{10}$$

One way to check them is to stick them in your <u>calculator</u>.

$\frac{2}{5} = 0.4$ and $\frac{4}{10} = 0.4$, so they're the <u>same</u>.

**EXAMPLE:**

$$\frac{18}{30} \xrightarrow{\div 6} \frac{3}{5}$$

$\frac{18}{30} = 0.6$ and $\frac{3}{5} = 0.6$

So, they're the same too.

Or you can use <u>fraction bars</u>:

It's obvious really — if I divide a bar of chocolate into 4 equal pieces, and I scoff 2 of them, it's the same as if there were two bits and I had one of them.

$\frac{1}{2}$

$\frac{2}{4}$

...and see that the <u>same</u> <u>amount</u> is shaded.

# Fractions

## Which Is The Biggest?

There are three different ways to find which out of a load of fractions is the biggest.

### Comparing Fractions

**Method 1)** Convert to decimals and put them in order (see pages 22 & 34).

**Method 2)** Use fraction bars and see which has the most shading.

**Method 3)** If the denominators are the same, all you have to do is compare the numerators — when it's bigger, the fraction's bigger. If the denominators are different, you can make them the same by finding equivalent fractions.

**EXAMPLE:** Put $\frac{1}{3}$, $\frac{1}{4}$ and $\frac{2}{5}$ in order, starting with the biggest.

**ANSWER:** I'm going to use method 1 by changing them into decimals.

$$\frac{1}{3} = 0.33, \qquad \frac{1}{4} = 0.25, \qquad \frac{2}{5} = 0.4$$

0.4 is the biggest, then 0.33, then 0.25. So the order is: $\frac{2}{5}$, $\frac{1}{3}$, $\frac{1}{4}$.

**EXAMPLE:** Put $\frac{3}{8}$, $\frac{7}{8}$ and $\frac{4}{8}$ in order, starting with the smallest.

**ANSWER:** We're in luck. All the denominators are the same, so we can use method 3. 7 is biggest, followed by 4, followed by 3. But watch out — this time they asked for the smallest first, the sneaky tricksters. So it's $\frac{3}{8}$, $\frac{4}{8}$, $\frac{7}{8}$.

**EXAMPLE:** Put $\frac{5}{6}$, $\frac{1}{2}$ and $\frac{2}{3}$ in order, starting with the smallest.

**ANSWER:** We can use equivalent fractions to make the denominators of these fractions the same, then we can compare them using method 3.

$$\frac{1}{2} \xrightarrow{\times 3} \frac{3}{6} \qquad \frac{2}{3} \xrightarrow{\times 2} \frac{4}{6}$$

$\frac{1}{2} = \frac{3}{6}$ and $\frac{2}{3} = \frac{4}{6}$. We can compare $\frac{5}{6}$, $\frac{3}{6}$ and $\frac{4}{6}$ by comparing numerators.

3 is smallest, then 4, then 5, so the order is $\frac{3}{6}$, $\frac{4}{6}$, $\frac{5}{6}$.

Using the original fractions from the question, that's $\frac{1}{2}$, $\frac{2}{3}$, $\frac{5}{6}$.

## Wine bars, Burger bars... Fraction bars?

1) Draw fraction bars for $\frac{2}{5}$, $\frac{1}{3}$ and $\frac{9}{10}$.

2) Pick out the equivalent fractions from this list: $\frac{6}{9}$, $\frac{11}{55}$, $\frac{2}{3}$, $\frac{3}{4}$, $\frac{21}{28}$, $\frac{1}{5}$.

3) Put these in order, starting with the smallest: $\frac{1}{3}$, $\frac{2}{5}$, $\frac{1}{2}$.

# Division and Fractions

## You Can Use Fractions Instead of Remainders

If you do a division where the number you're dividing by won't go exactly, you end up with a bit left over, or a "remainder". Using fractions you can divide the remainder too.

**EXAMPLE:** Find 17 ÷ 5.

**ANSWER:** 17 ÷ 5 = <u>3 remainder 2</u>
We've got a <u>remainder</u>, because 5 goes into 17 <u>3 times</u>, with 2 left over that won't divide by 5...
...but with <u>fractions</u> you <u>can</u> divide 2 by 5.
2 ÷ 5 is the same as the fraction $\frac{2}{5}$.
So 17 ÷ 5 = $3\frac{2}{5}$

Fraction Man to the rescue!

## You Can Turn Remainders Into Decimals Too

You can also use decimals in your answers to division questions instead of fractions.

**EXAMPLE:** Find 29 ÷ 10.

**ANSWER:** 29 ÷ 10 = <u>2 remainder 9</u>
9 ÷ 10 is the same as the fraction $\frac{9}{10}$.
So 29 ÷ 10 = $2\frac{9}{10}$.
$\frac{9}{10}$ is the same as the decimal 0.9, so 29 ÷ 10 = 2.9.

Doctor Decimal

**EXAMPLE:** Beth buys a 50 cm-long giant chocolate bar.
She decides to share it equally between herself and 3 friends.
How many cm of chocolate bar does each person get?

**ANSWER:** The 50 cm chocolate bar is being shared between <u>4 people</u>.
So we need to find <u>50 ÷ 4</u>.

50 ÷ 4 = <u>12 remainder 2</u>

2 ÷ 4 is the same as the fraction $\frac{2}{4} = \frac{1}{2} = 0.5$.

So each friend gets 50 cm ÷ 4 = $12\frac{1}{2}$ cm = 12.5 cm.

## Remainders — like rounders, but with less running...

1) Give the answers to the following, using fractions for the remainders.
   a) 7 ÷ 2    b) 25 ÷ 4    c) 33 ÷ 10    d) 20 ÷ 3    e) 48 ÷ 7
2) Ron has 41 litres of juice, which he shares equally between 5 containers.
   How much juice goes into each container? Give your answer using fractions,
   then rewrite it using decimals.

# *Percentages*

## *"Per Cent" Means "Out of 100"*

% is a short way of writing <u>per cent</u>.
So 20% is twenty per cent, which is 20 <u>out of 100</u>.

## *Some Common Ones You'd Better Know*

Make sure you <u>learn these</u> because they come up all the time:

$\frac{1}{2}$ is the same as 0.5, which is the same as 50%.

$\frac{1}{4}$ is the same as 0.25, which is the same as 25%.

$\frac{3}{4}$ is the same as 0.75, which is the same as 75%.

$\frac{1}{1}$ is the same as 1, which is the same as 100%.

Converting to decimals and fractions is easy. If you get some of these in your tests then you're <u>laughing</u>... if you've learnt how to do them.

## *Converting to Decimals Is Really Easy*

### % to Decimals

1) All you do is <u>divide by 100</u>.

2) Check out page 26 to see that that just means moving the digits <u>two places to the right</u>.

3) It's the easiest thing in the <u>Universe</u>.

### Decimals to %

1) Is just the <u>opposite</u>.

2) So you <u>times by 100</u>.

3) That means all you have to do is move the digits <u>two places to the left</u>.

4) It's a doddle.

**EXAMPLE:** a) Convert 26% to a decimal.
b) Convert 0.85 to a percentage.

<u>ANSWER:</u> a) 26% = 26 ÷ 100 = 0.26.
b) 0.85 × 100 = 85%.

**ANOTHER EXAMPLE:**

a) 98% of cats like the taste of mouse. Convert 98% to a decimal.

b) 0.25 of mice like the taste of cat. Convert 0.25 to a percentage.

<u>ANSWER:</u> a) 98% = 98 ÷ 100 = 0.98.
b) 0.25 × 100 = 25%.

# Percentages

## Converting Percentages to Fractions

### % to Fractions

1) It's even easier.

2) A percentage is always "out of 100".

3) So all you do is write the percentage as the top, and 100 as the bottom of the fraction.

**EXAMPLE:**

Convert 47% to a fraction.

**ANSWER:** 47 goes at the top.

$$\frac{47}{100}$$

100 goes at the bottom.

Hey - it's all just too easy for me.

**EXAMPLE:** 3% of astronauts would rather spend their holidays in Barrow-on-Sea than on Jupiter. What fraction is this?

**ANSWER:** 3 goes at the top.

$$\frac{3}{100}$$ 100 goes at the bottom.

## Fractions to Percentages — Slightly Trickier

Converting fractions to percentages is a tiny bit harder, but let's face it, how easy do you want these pages to be?

### Fractions to %

1) All you have to do is convert the fraction to a decimal first.

2) I'd use a calculator if I were doing it.

3) Then turn it into a percentage like before.

**EXAMPLE:**

Write $\frac{39}{150}$ as a percentage.

**ANSWER:**

Using a calculator,
$39 \div 150 = 0.26$ (decimal).
Now turn it into a percentage...
$0.26 \times 100 = 26\%$.

**EXAMPLE:** Last year, Frank's racing camel won $\frac{30}{200}$ of the races it entered.

Hank's racing goose won $\frac{28}{175}$ of its races last year.

Which animal won the bigger percentage of races?

**ANSWER:** Start with Frank's camel.
Decimal first — get out the calculator. $30 \div 200 = 0.15$
Turn it into a percentage... $0.15 \times 100 = \underline{15\%}$.
Now do the same for Hank's goose. The decimal is $28 \div 175 = 0.16$
Turn it into a percentage... $0.16 \times 100 = \underline{16\%}$.
So Hank's goose won a bigger percentage of races than Frank's camel last year.

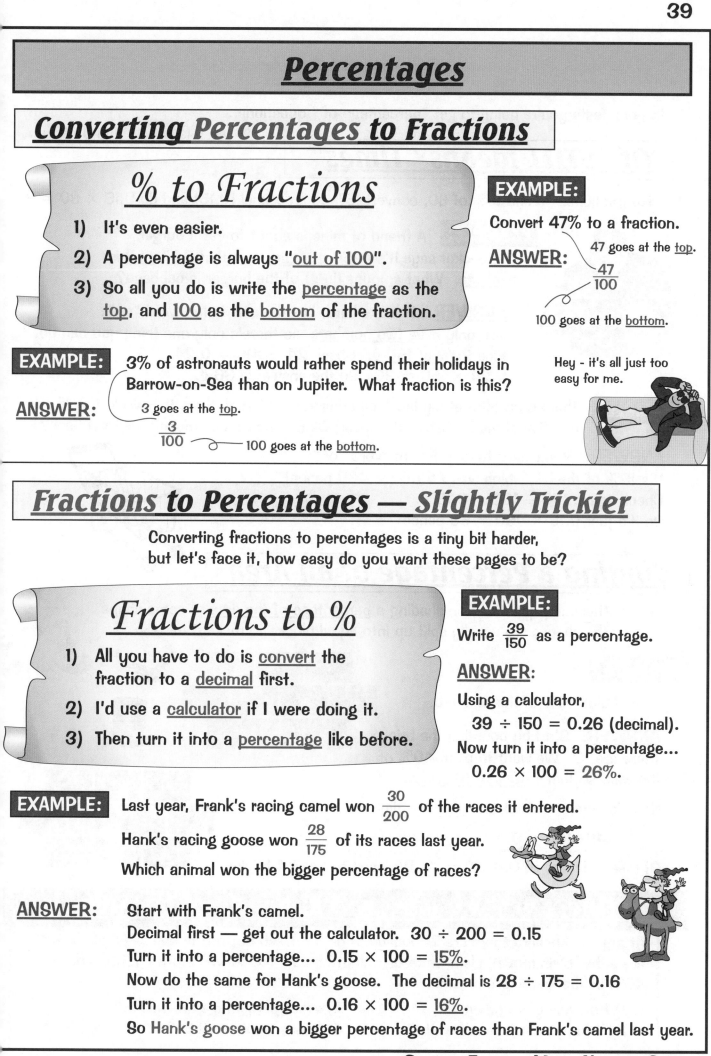

# Percentages

In your Tests you're going to get "percentage of" questions...

so this is how you do them.

## "Of" STILL means "Times"

It's like fractions. To find 15% of 60, convert 15% to a decimal (0.15) and do 0.15 × 60 = 9.

**EXAMPLE:** A friend of mine is about to eat a burger. The packet says it's a <u>150 g burger</u>, and that <u>24% of it</u> is <u>cabbage</u>. What <u>amount (in g)</u> of the burger is cabbage?

<u>ANSWER</u>: It looks hard, but the clue is the word "of". You only have <u>two numbers</u>, so there's only one thing you can do. Find <u>24% of 150 g</u>. Check 24 ÷ 100 = 0.24. 0.24 × 150 = 36. So the answer is 36 g.

**EXAMPLE:** There is an offer at my local supermarket. If I shop there this week, they'll give me 15% of my bill back. If I spend £4.60, how much money will I get back?

<u>ANSWER</u>: Remember to look for the word "of". It's 15% of the bill, which was £4.60 (or 460 pence). Check again... 15 ÷ 100 = 0.15. So it's just 0.15 × 460 = 69 pence.

## Finding a Percentage of an Area

These are questions on shading a <u>percentage of the area</u> of some shape. The shapes are usually split up into equal blocks to make it easier.

**EXAMPLE:**

Paint 40% of this wall red.

<u>ANSWER</u>: Start by counting the bricks. There are 10. We want to paint 40% of the wall, so that's <u>40% of 10 bricks</u>.

No calculators allowed, so <u>move the digits</u>:

40÷100 = 0.4

Of means times, so 0.4×10 = 4. We need to paint 4 bricks.

## Segatnecrep — so easy you know them backwards...

At my local bakery there are 20 loaves of bread, fresh out of the oven. All of them are either plain brown, plain white or walnut bread. Two loaves are walnut bread. 40% of the loaves are brown.

1) How many are brown?          2) What percentage are walnut?

3) What percentage are white?          4) How many are white?

# Estimating Fractions and Percentages

## You Can Estimate Fractions and Percentages

Even if you don't have any numbers to work with, fractions and percentages can still be useful for describing real-life situations.

**EXAMPLE:** Edward and Edwina went to a fancy restaurant and ordered giant hotdogs.

**A GIANT HOTDOG**          **EDWARD'S PLATE**          **EDWINA'S PLATE**

Estimate what fraction of his hotdog Edward has left on his plate, and what fraction of her hotdog Edwina has left on her plate.

**ANSWER:** Compare the length of Edward's bit of hotdog to the length of a full one. About 2 of these bits would be the same length as one full hotdog.

So Edward has about $\frac{1}{2}$ of a hotdog left.

Edwina's got a smaller bit of hotdog left. You'd need about 3 bits like this to make one hotdog.

So Edwina has about $\frac{1}{3}$ of a hotdog left.

**EXAMPLE:** On the gameshow "Cow or Spaceship," winners spin this wheel to find out what prize they get. Estimate what percentage of the wheel is made up of "cow" sections.

**ANSWER:** There are 5 sections on the wheel. They're not exactly the same size,

but they each take up about $\frac{1}{5}$ of the wheel.

There are 2 cow sections, so that's about $\frac{2}{5}$ of the wheel. Now we just need to turn that into a percentage.
Convert the fraction to a decimal:   $2 \div 5 = 0.4$
Then convert the decimal to a pecentage:     $0.4 \times 100 = 40\%$
About 40% of the wheel is made up of "cow" sections.

## I estimate you enjoyed 100% of this page...

This is the logo of the Fraction and Percentage Estimation Company Ltd.
1)   Estimate what fraction of the logo is coloured blue.
2)   Estimate what percentage of the logo is coloured yellow.

# Ratio and Proportion

## Ratios Compare One Part to Another Part

Take a look at this pattern:

You can describe this as a <u>ratio</u>.  For the 2 white boxes there are 6 red boxes.
In other words <u>for every white box there are 3 red boxes</u>.  The ratio is <u>1 white to 3 red</u>.
The ratio compares the number of <u>white</u> boxes to the number of <u>red</u> boxes.

The questions you'll get on this might ask you to use a ratio to solve a simple problem...

**EXAMPLE:**  For every 5 takeaway pizzas Simon buys, he gets 1 free healthy salad.
If he buys 20 pizzas, how many free healthy salads does he get?

**ANSWER:**  The ratio is <u>5 pizzas to 1 salad</u>.  To get from 5 pizzas to 20 pizzas you <u>multiply by 4</u>.
You need to do the same to the number of salads — 1 × 4 = <u>4 free healthy salads</u>.

## Proportions Compare a Part to the Whole Thing

Look again at the pattern at the top of the page.  You can also describe it with <u>proportions</u>.
In the 8 boxes there are 6 red boxes and 2 white boxes.
In other words <u>in every 4 boxes there are 3 red boxes and 1 white box</u>.

The proportion of red boxes is <u>3 in every 4</u>.  The proportion of white boxes is <u>1 in every 4</u>.
The proportion compares the number of <u>red</u> or <u>white</u> boxes to the <u>total</u> number of boxes.

Proportions are really another way of writing fractions.
The proportion "1 in every 4" is the same as the fraction $\frac{1}{4}$.

**EXAMPLE:**  The picture shows Geraldine's fish bowl.
What proportion of the fish are pink?

**ANSWER:**  There are <u>9 fish</u> in total, and <u>3 of them</u> are pink.
So the proportion of fish that are pink is <u>3 in every 9</u>.
That's the same as <u>1 in every 3</u>.

**EXAMPLE:**  The proportion of wasp truffles in each box of Chorlton's Chocolates is 1 in every 6.
If Tony buys a box of 30 chocolates, how many wasp truffles will he get?

**ANSWER:**
There's <u>1 wasp truffle</u> in every <u>6 chocolates</u>, so we need to know
<u>how many 6's</u> there are in Tony's box of 30:  <u>30 ÷ 6 = 5</u>.
There are 5 lots of 6 chocolates in the box, so to get the number of wasp
truffles, multiply <u>1 by 5</u>.  So Tony gets 1 × 5 = <u>5 wasp truffles</u>.

## Professionals eat five pro-portions of fruit a day...

1) In Geraldine's fish bowl from the example above, find the ratio of:
   a) green fish to non-green fish      b) blue fish to non-blue fish
2) The proportion of spaghetti trees in my orchard is 1 in every 4.
   If there are 32 trees in the orchard, how many spaghetti trees do I have?

# Multiples

## Multiples are Just Like Times Tables

So the <u>multiples of 2</u> are just the numbers in the <u>2 times table</u>:

2   4   6   8   10   12   14   16   ...

> It's easy to remember:
> MULTIPLEs are just
> MULTIPLication tables.

| The <u>multiples of 8</u> are | 8 | 16 | 24 | 32 | 40 | 48 | ... |
|---|---|---|---|---|---|---|---|
| The <u>multiples of 6</u> are | 6 | 12 | 18 | 24 | 30 | 36 | 42 ... |
| The <u>multiples of 12</u> are | 12 | 24 | 36 | 48 | 60 | 72 | 84 ... |

## The Last Digit

Some multiples are easier to spot than others.  Have a look at the <u>multiples of 10</u>:

10   20   30   40   50   60   ...

> They all end in <u>zero</u>.

It's nearly the same for 5:

5   10   15   20   25   30   ...

> They all end in <u>five or zero</u>.

and again for 2:

> They all end in
> <u>0, 2, 4, 6, or 8</u>

2   4   6   8   10   12   14   16   18   20   ...

**EXAMPLES:**   50 <u>ends in zero</u>, so it's a multiple of 2, a multiple of 5 and a multiple of 10.
175 <u>ends in five</u>, so it's a multiple of 5.
364 <u>ends in four</u>, so it's a multiple of 2.

## Finding Multiples — Use a Calculator

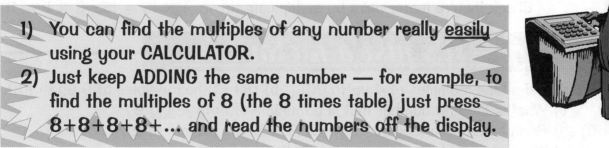

1) You can find the multiples of any number really <u>easily</u> using your CALCULATOR.
2) Just keep ADDING the same number — for example, to find the multiples of 8 (the 8 times table) just press 8+8+8+8+... and read the numbers off the display.

# Factors

## Factors are just "The Numbers that Divide into Something"

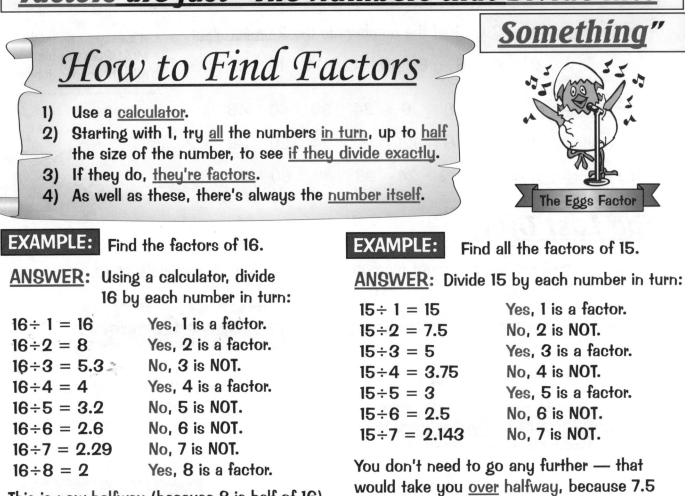

### How to Find Factors

1) Use a <u>calculator</u>.
2) Starting with 1, try <u>all</u> the numbers <u>in turn</u>, up to <u>half</u> the size of the number, to see <u>if they divide exactly</u>.
3) If they do, <u>they're factors</u>.
4) As well as these, there's always the <u>number itself</u>.

The Eggs Factor

---

**EXAMPLE:** Find the factors of 16.

**ANSWER:** Using a calculator, divide 16 by each number in turn:

| | |
|---|---|
| $16 \div 1 = 16$ | Yes, 1 is a factor. |
| $16 \div 2 = 8$ | Yes, 2 is a factor. |
| $16 \div 3 = 5.3$ | No, 3 is NOT. |
| $16 \div 4 = 4$ | Yes, 4 is a factor. |
| $16 \div 5 = 3.2$ | No, 5 is NOT. |
| $16 \div 6 = 2.6$ | No, 6 is NOT. |
| $16 \div 7 = 2.29$ | No, 7 is NOT. |
| $16 \div 8 = 2$ | Yes, 8 is a factor. |

This is now <u>halfway</u> (because 8 is half of 16) so we can **STOP**. So the factors of 16 are 1, 2, 4, 8, and <u>16 itself</u> don't forget.

---

**EXAMPLE:** Find all the factors of 15.

**ANSWER:** Divide 15 by each number in turn:

| | |
|---|---|
| $15 \div 1 = 15$ | Yes, 1 is a factor. |
| $15 \div 2 = 7.5$ | No, 2 is NOT. |
| $15 \div 3 = 5$ | Yes, 3 is a factor. |
| $15 \div 4 = 3.75$ | No, 4 is NOT. |
| $15 \div 5 = 3$ | Yes, 5 is a factor. |
| $15 \div 6 = 2.5$ | No, 6 is NOT. |
| $15 \div 7 = 2.143$ | No, 7 is NOT. |

You don't need to go any further — that would take you <u>over</u> halfway, because 7.5 is half of 15.
So the factors of 15 are 1, 3, 5 and 15.

---

## You Can Write Factors as Factor Pairs

<u>Factor pairs</u> multiply together to give the number. The <u>smallest factor</u> makes a pair with the <u>biggest one</u>, the <u>second smallest</u> makes a pair with the <u>second biggest</u>, and so on. If there are an odd number of factors, you have to multiply the <u>middle factor</u> by itself — so it's not part of a factor pair.

**EXAMPLE:** The factors of 15 are 1, 3, 5 and 15.
So the factor pairs for 15 are 1 and 15, and 3 and 5.
Check they're factor pairs by multiplying them: $1 \times 15 = 15$, $3 \times 5 = 15$

---

## Dividing — it's just a factor life...

1) a) List all the multiples of 4 up to 60.    b) List all the multiples of 9 up to 100.
   c) What is the first number that is a multiple of both 4 <u>and</u> 9?
2) a) Find all the factors of 6.    b) Find all the factors of 21.
   c) What two numbers are factors of both 6 and 21?

# Prime Numbers

Prime numbers can be <u>tricky</u>, but they're a <u>lot less tricky</u> if you just <u>learn</u> these basics:

## PRIME Numbers Only Have Two Factors

A <u>prime number</u> is a number that has exactly <u>TWO FACTORS</u> – 1 and <u>itself</u>.
Here are the first few prime numbers:

**2   3   5   7   11   13   17   19   23   29   31   37   ...**

As you can see, they're an <u>awkward-looking</u> bunch
The <u>only way</u> to get <u>any</u> prime number is: 1 × ITSELF.

### EXAMPLE:

The <u>only numbers</u> that multiply to give 11 are 1 × 11.
The <u>only numbers</u> that multiply to give 23 are 1 × 23.

*Work hard to get ahead.*

*But I've already got a head.*

## 1 is NOT a Prime Number — it Just Isn't

1) <u>1 is NOT a prime number</u> — it doesn't have exactly 2 factors,
   and prime numbers do.
2) The first 4 primes are <u>2, 3, 5 and 7</u>.
3) <u>2 and 5 are the EXCEPTIONS</u> because all the rest end in <u>1, 3, 7 or 9</u>.
4) But <u>NOT ALL</u> numbers ending in 1, 3, 7 or 9 are primes, as shown here:
   (Only the circled ones are primes.)

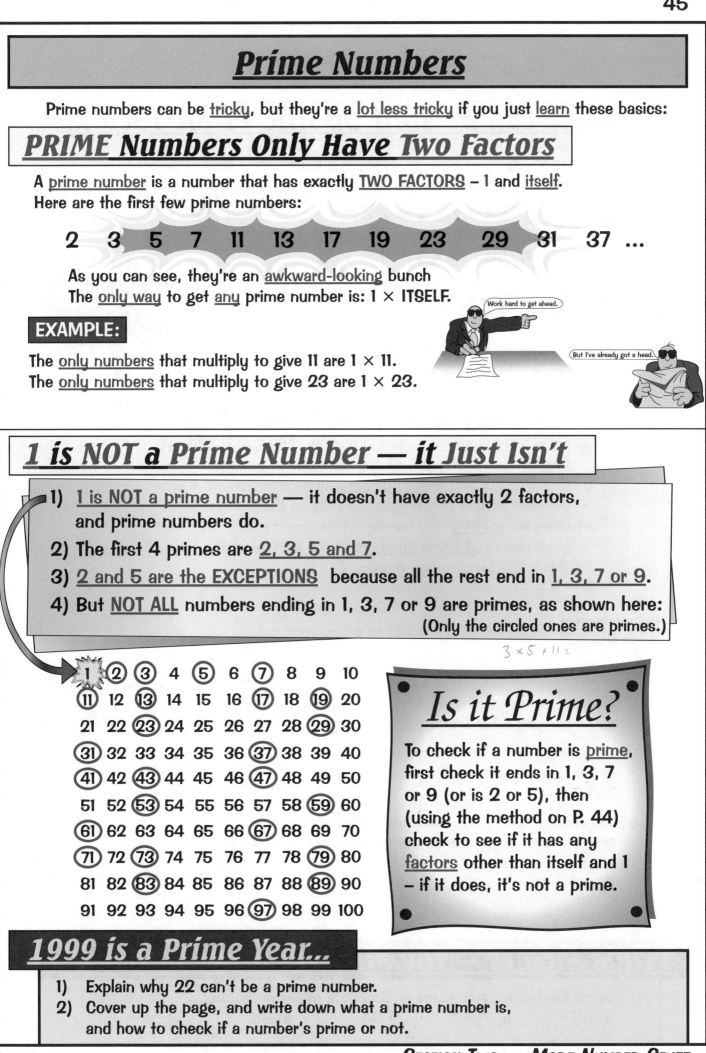

3 × 5 × 11 =

① ② ③ 4 ⑤ 6 ⑦ 8 9 10
⑪ 12 ⑬ 14 15 16 ⑰ 18 ⑲ 20
21 22 ㉓ 24 25 26 27 28 ㉙ 30
㉛ 32 33 34 35 36 ㊲ 38 39 40
㊶ 42 ㊸ 44 45 46 ㊼ 48 49 50
51 52 ㊾ 54 55 56 57 58 ㊾ 60
㊽ 62 63 64 65 66 ㊿ 68 69 70
㋒ 72 ㋓ 74 75 76 77 78 ㋓ 80
81 82 ㋓ 84 85 86 87 88 ㋓ 90
91 92 93 94 95 96 ㋓ 98 99 100

### Is it Prime?

To check if a number is <u>prime</u>,
first check it ends in 1, 3, 7
or 9 (or is 2 or 5), then
(using the method on P. 44)
check to see if it has any
<u>factors</u> other than itself and 1
– if it does, it's not a prime.

## 1999 is a Prime Year...

1) Explain why 22 can't be a prime number.
2) Cover up the page, and write down what a prime number is,
   and how to check if a number's prime or not.

# Prime Factors

## Numbers Can Be Split Up Into Prime Factors

You can write any number as a list of prime numbers multiplied together.
This is called writing a number as a product of prime factors.

**EXAMPLES:**
1) $24 = 2 \times 2 \times 2 \times 3$
2) $35 = 5 \times 7$
3) $99 = 3 \times 3 \times 11$

## The Factor Tree

To split a number into prime factors,
you can use the Factor Tree method.

1) Start by writing the number at the top of the page.
2) Draw two branches below the number, and split it into two factors, one at the end of each branch.
3) If you've got any prime numbers, draw a ring round them. Because they're prime, you can't divide them any more.
4) Carry on splitting any numbers that aren't prime, until you get a row of all prime numbers at the bottom of the page. This is the list of prime factors.

**EXAMPLE:** Write 42 as a product of prime factors.

**ANSWER:**

1) I've started by splitting 42 into $2 \times 21$, but you could use any other factor pair that makes 42.

2) Put a ring around the 2, because it's prime. We need to divide the 21 again, because it isn't prime.

3) 21 divides into $3 \times 7$. These are both prime. Now we've only got prime numbers at the bottom of the factor tree.
So $42 = 2 \times 3 \times 7$

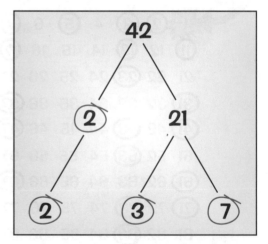

## Prime factors — the answers grow on trees...

1) Write the following numbers as products of prime factors:
   a) 88      b) 75      c) 54      d) 96      e) 84

# Even & Odd Numbers

There are <u>four</u> special types of numbers that you should <u>know</u>:

## Even Numbers

2  4  6  8  10  12  14  16  18  20 ...

*In other words the <u>2 times table</u>.*

All EVEN numbers end with a 0, 2, 4, 6 or 8.

**EXAMPLE:**  344, 690, 18, 6 and 1732 are all even numbers, because they all end in 0, 2, 4, 6 or 8.

## Odd Numbers

1  3  5  7  9  11  13  15  17  19  21 ...

*<u>All</u> whole numbers are either <u>even</u> or <u>odd</u>.*

All ODD numbers end with either a 1, 3, 5, 7 or 9.

**EXAMPLE:**  5, 911, 183, 257 and 79 are all odd numbers, because they all end in 1, 3, 5, 7 or 9.

# Some Useful Facts about Even & Odd Numbers:

1) Even numbers <u>all divide by 2</u> without a remainder.

2) Odd numbers all give a <u>remainder</u> when you divide by 2.

3) If you <u>add two</u> even numbers together you ALWAYS get an even number.

4) If you <u>add two</u> odd numbers together you ALWAYS get an even number.

5) If you <u>add</u> an even number and an odd number you ALWAYS get an odd number.

**EXAMPLES:**

1)  $26 \div 2 = 13$

2)  $57 \div 2 = 28$ rem 1

3)  $36 + 8 = 44$

4)  $13 + 27 = 40$

5)  $41 + 16 = 57$
    $20 + 31 = 51$

*It doesn't matter which order you add them in.*

## ODD numbers? — I reckon all numbers are weird...

Learn what EVEN and ODD numbers are. Turn the page and write the first 10 of each.

Pick out   1) all the even numbers  and  2) all the odd numbers from this list:

27,    49,    100,    81,    125,    31,    132,    50

# Square Numbers

## Square Numbers

When a number is multiplied by itself, the result is a __SQUARE NUMBER__.

| 1 | 4 | 9 | 16 | 25 | 36 | 49 | 64 | 81 | 100 | 121 | 144... |
|---|---|---|---|---|---|---|---|---|---|---|---|
| (1×1) | (2×2) | (3×3) | (4×4) | (5×5) | (6×6) | (7×7) | (8×8) | (9×9) | (10×10) | (11×11) | (12×12)... |

They're called <u>square numbers</u> because they
are like the areas of this pattern of squares.

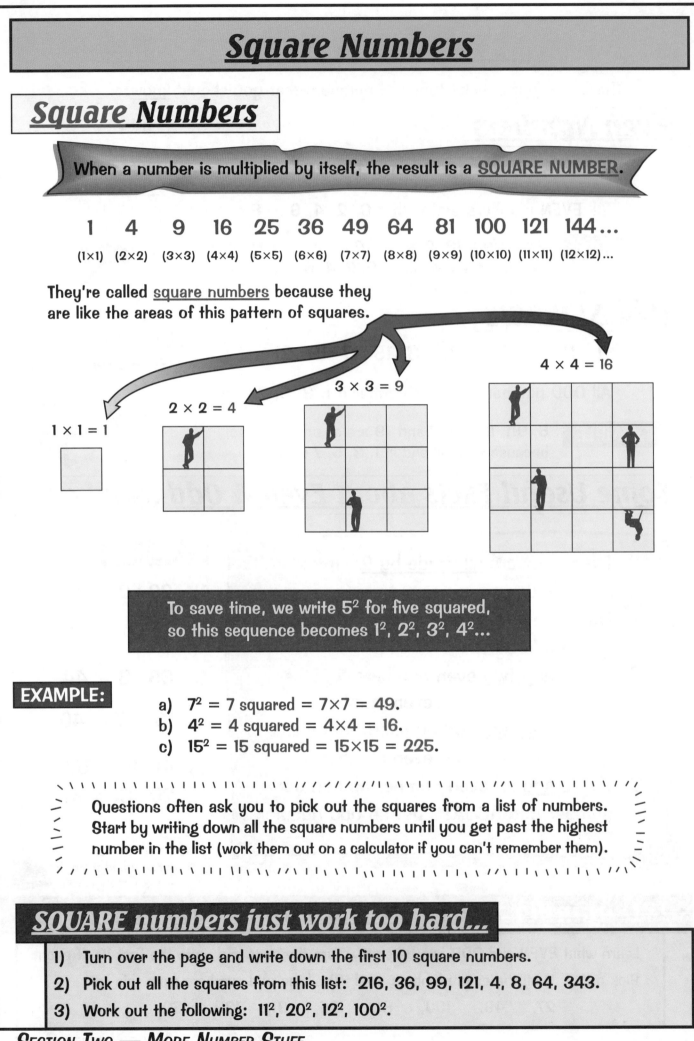

$1 \times 1 = 1$

$2 \times 2 = 4$

$3 \times 3 = 9$

$4 \times 4 = 16$

To save time, we write $5^2$ for five squared,
so this sequence becomes $1^2$, $2^2$, $3^2$, $4^2$...

**EXAMPLE:**

a)  $7^2$ = 7 squared = 7×7 = **49**.
b)  $4^2$ = 4 squared = 4×4 = **16**.
c)  $15^2$ = 15 squared = 15×15 = **225**.

Questions often ask you to pick out the squares from a list of numbers.
Start by writing down all the square numbers until you get past the highest
number in the list (work them out on a calculator if you can't remember them).

## SQUARE numbers just work too hard...

1)  Turn over the page and write down the first 10 square numbers.

2)  Pick out all the squares from this list:  216, 36, 99, 121, 4, 8, 64, 343.

3)  Work out the following:  $11^2$, $20^2$, $12^2$, $100^2$.

# Calculators (2)

## If You Press the Wrong Button

Don't panic — if you type the wrong number DON'T jump straight for the AC button. The DEL button (or C button on old-style calculators) will cancel the number you just typed in, then you can carry on.

**EXAMPLE:** You are trying to work out $32 \times 54$, which means you've got to type

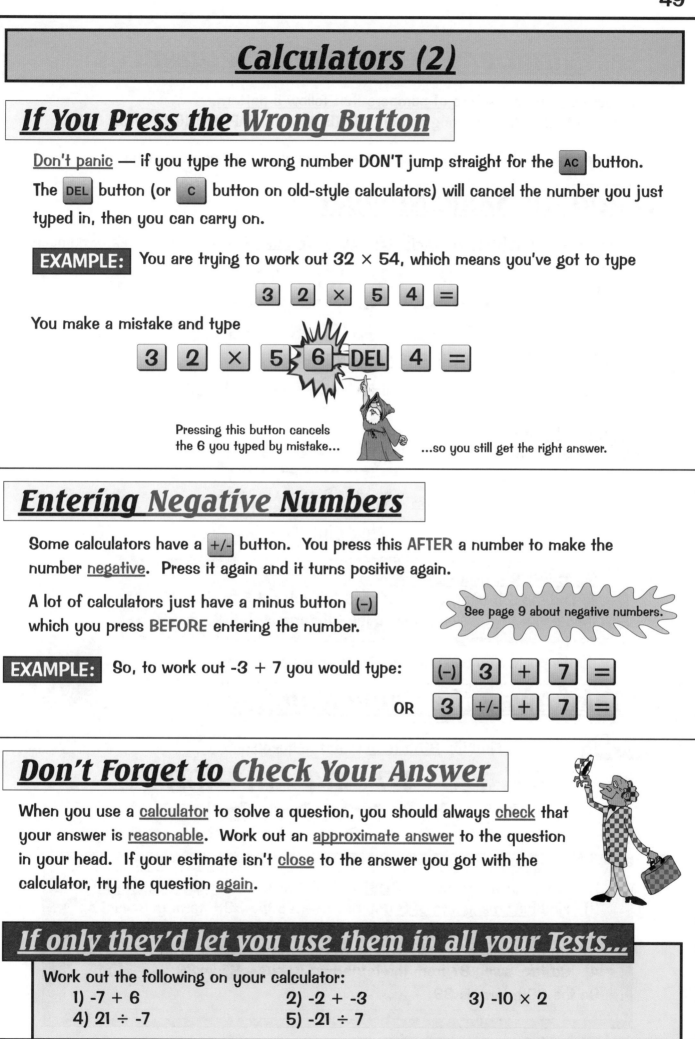

[ 3 ] [ 2 ] [ × ] [ 5 ] [ 4 ] [ = ]

You make a mistake and type

[ 3 ] [ 2 ] [ × ] [ 5 ] [ 6 ] [ DEL ] [ 4 ] [ = ]

Pressing this button cancels
the 6 you typed by mistake...          ...so you still get the right answer.

## Entering Negative Numbers

Some calculators have a +/- button. You press this AFTER a number to make the number *negative*. Press it again and it turns positive again.

A lot of calculators just have a minus button (-) which you press BEFORE entering the number.

See page 9 about negative numbers.

**EXAMPLE:** So, to work out $-3 + 7$ you would type: [ (-) ] [ 3 ] [ + ] [ 7 ] [ = ]

OR [ 3 ] [ +/- ] [ + ] [ 7 ] [ = ]

## Don't Forget to Check Your Answer

When you use a <u>calculator</u> to solve a question, you should always <u>check</u> that your answer is <u>reasonable</u>. Work out an <u>approximate answer</u> to the question in your head. If your estimate isn't <u>close</u> to the answer you got with the calculator, try the question <u>again</u>.

## If only they'd let you use them in all your Tests...

Work out the following on your calculator:
- 1) $-7 + 6$
- 2) $-2 + -3$
- 3) $-10 \times 2$
- 4) $21 \div -7$
- 5) $-21 \div 7$

# Number Patterns and Sequences

Number sequences are lists of numbers that follow a pattern.
They're not difficult — as long as you WRITE WHAT'S HAPPENING IN EACH GAP.

These are the six different types of number sequences they could give you.

## 1) Add the Same Number

The SECRET is to WRITE THE DIFFERENCES IN THE GAPS between each pair of numbers:

**EXAMPLE:**

**3   8   13   18   23** ...

+5    +5    +5    +5    +5

So the RULE is "ADD 5 TO THE PREVIOUS NUMBER".

Once you know this, you can use it to find other terms — the 6th term is 23 + 5 = 28.

Now look a bit closer —
To find the 6th term the sum was 3 + 5 + 5 + 5 + 5 + 5 = 28

This number is always 1 less than this one

Here are 5 lots of 5.
That's just 5 × 5...

> **SO THERE'S A QUICKER WAY —**
> To find the 6th term, you only need to work out 5 × 5 = 25,
> then add it to 3. Which means the 6th term is 3 + 25 = 28.

The handy thing is... you can use it for subtracting terms too.

## 2) Take Away the Same Number

**EXAMPLE:**        Find the 30th term in this sequence.

**123   120   117   114   111   108** ...

– 3     – 3     – 3     – 3     – 3     – 3

1)  Work out the RULE — "SUBTRACT 3 FROM THE PREVIOUS TERM".
2)  Find how many lots of 3 you need — it's the 30th term you want so you take away one less than thirty lots, which is 29 lots.
3)  Do the times bit — 29 × 3 = 87.
4)  So take away 87 from the 1st term:      123 – 87 = 36.
So the 30th term is 36.

I didn't mean that sort of takeaway...

# Number Patterns and Sequences

## 3) Add or Subtract a Changing Number

Again, <u>WRITE THE CHANGE IN THE GAPS</u>, as shown here:

**EXAMPLE:**

2   4   7   11   16   ...

+2   +3   +4   +5   +6

30   23   17   12   8   ...

− 7   − 6   − 5   − 4   − 3

The <u>RULE</u>: "Add 1 <u>EXTRA</u> each time to the <u>previous term</u>."      "Subtract 1 <u>EXTRA</u> from the <u>previous term</u>."

## 4) Multiply by the Same Number Each Time

This type has a common <u>MULTIPLIER</u> linking each pair of numbers:

**EXAMPLE:**

2   4   8   16   ...

×2   ×2   ×2   ×2

4   12   36   108   ...

×3   ×3   ×3   ×3

The <u>RULE</u>:      "Multiply the <u>previous term</u> by 2."      "Multiply the <u>previous term</u> by 3."

## 5) Divide by the Same Number Each Time

This type has the same <u>DIVIDER</u> between each pair of numbers:

**EXAMPLE:**

400   200   100   50   ...

÷2   ÷2   ÷2   ÷2

70 000   7000   700   70   ...

÷10   ÷10   ÷10   ÷10

The <u>RULE</u>:      "Divide the <u>previous term</u> by 2."      "Divide the <u>previous term</u> by 10."

## 6) Add the Previous Two Terms

This type of sequence works by adding the last two numbers to get the next one:

**EXAMPLE:**

1   1   2   3   5   8   13   ...

1+1   1+2   2+3   3+5   5+8   8+13

The <u>RULE</u>:      "Add the previous two terms."

## So what's "Autumn Term + Spring Term" then?

1) Write down the next 3 terms and the 15th term of these sequences:
   a)  21, 25, 29, 33, 37, ...      b)  200, 191, 182, 173, 164, ...
2) Write the next 3 terms of these sequences: a) 11, 33, 99, ...  b) 1600, 800, 400, ...
3) Write down the 8th term in this sequence: 1, 1, 2, 3, 5, 8, 13, ...

# Number Patterns and Sequences

## A Typical Question is...

What we're going to look at is a...

"State the rule for extending the pattern"

...type of question.

This is what a lot of <u>Test questions</u> end up asking for and it's easy enough so long as you remember this:

> With Number Patterns <u>always</u> say what you do to the <u>previous term</u> to get the <u>next term</u>.

All the number sequences on the last page have the rule for extending the pattern written underneath them. Notice that they all refer to the <u>term that came before</u>.

<u>BUT</u>: You won't always be given a number pattern as a string of numbers.

In fact, more often they'll start by giving you a <u>series of picture patterns</u> instead.

## ...How Many Sprouts?

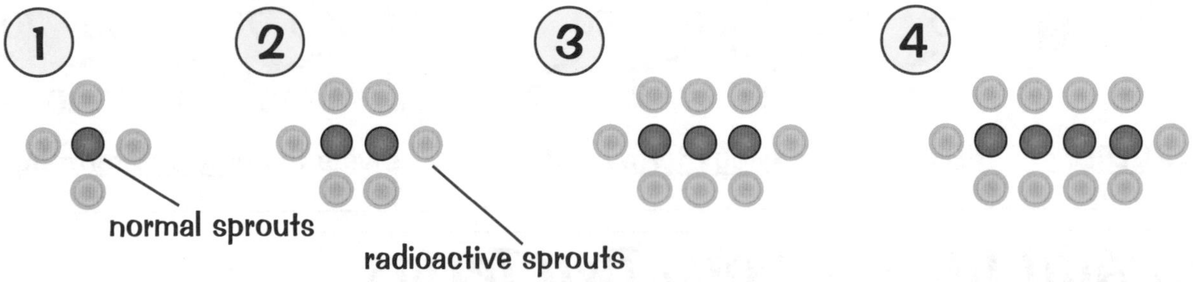

① ② ③ ④

normal sprouts

radioactive sprouts

You might be asked, "How many sprouts (in total) will be in pattern number ⑤ ?"

Just turn it into a <u>number</u> sequence and you'll get the answer soon enough:

| ① | ② | ③ | ④ | ⑤ |
|---|---|---|---|---|
| 5 sprouts | 8 sprouts | 11 sprouts | 14 sprouts | 17 sprouts |

+3    +3    +3    +3

# Number Patterns and Sequences

## ...Or How Many Worms?

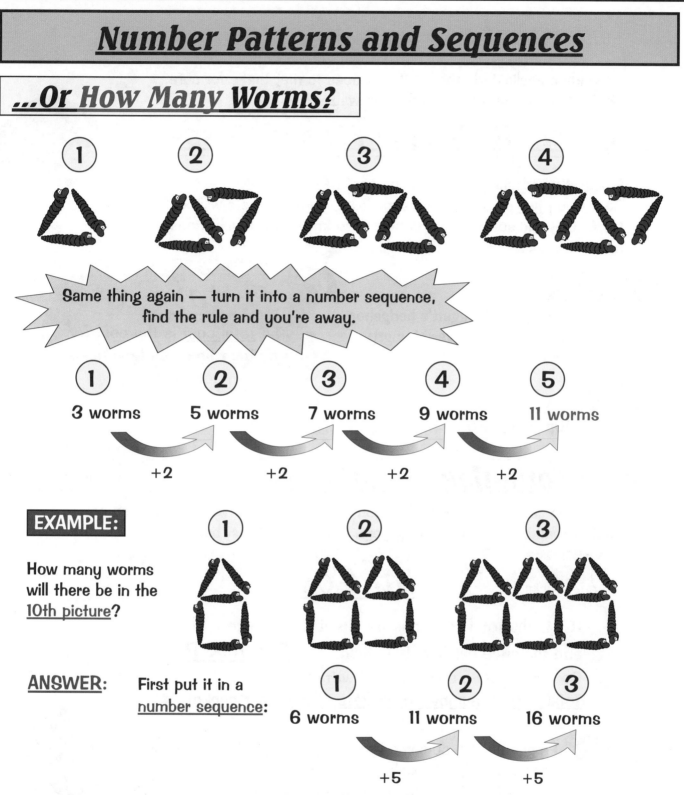

Same thing again — turn it into a number sequence, find the rule and you're away.

① 3 worms   ② 5 worms   ③ 7 worms   ④ 9 worms   ⑤ 11 worms

+2   +2   +2   +2

**EXAMPLE:**

How many worms will there be in the 10th picture?

**ANSWER:**  First put it in a number sequence:

① 6 worms   ② 11 worms   ③ 16 worms

+5   +5

By the time we get to the 10th picture, we'll have added 9 lots of 5 worms to the 6 worms in the first picture.
So, we need to add 9 × 5 = 45 worms.
Which means the 10th picture will have 6 + 45 = 51 worms.

## It's no use trying to worm your way out of it...

1) Write down the rule for getting the number of radioactive sprouts in the series of patterns on the last page.

2) How many radioactive sprouts will there be in the: a) 5th picture;   b) 6th picture?

# *Word Formulae and Equations*

Sounds complicated, doesn't it?  It does to me, that's for sure.
But it isn't as bad as it sounds.  No way.

## *Froggatt's Hedgehog Flavour Crisps*

Froggatt's hedgehog flavour crisps cost 35p a packet.
So if I buy <u>two</u> packets it costs me 70p.  <u>Three</u> packets will cost me 105p
(or £1.05) and so on.  So if you want to know how much it costs
to buy a number of packets, it's just

**EXAMPLE:**

If I buy <u>4 packets</u> of Froggatt's hedgehog
flavour crisps because I'm very hungry,
how much will it cost?

<u>ANSWER:</u>

It costs me <u>4 times 35p,</u>
which is 140p (or £1.40).

### *Total Cost*

The <u>total cost</u> is the cost for
one item times by how many
of them you buy.

## *Letter Formulae (Equations)*

Much the same thing, really, but you use <u>symbols</u> like × and = and so on,
and instead of words you use <u>letters</u>.  The rule for cost becomes:

> You say one formula but two
> (or more) formulae.

### *Total Cost*

If **T** is the total cost, n is the number of packets I buy,
and the price per item is P, then:     $\underline{T = n \times P}$
So this is just a short way of writing
<u>Total Cost</u> = <u>number of packets</u> × <u>price per packet</u>.

**EXAMPLE:**   Froggatt's also do some very tasty <u>elephant flavour peanuts</u>.
They cost 28p per pack.
Write a formula for the cost, C, of n packets.

<u>ANSWER</u> in words: The total cost is the number of packs times the price (28p)

<u>ANSWER</u> in letters: Cost = number of packs × 28p, or **C = n × 28.**

**EXAMPLE:**   Froggatt's board of directors has 1999 people on it, but there are always some off sick
All of them attend meetings if they're not ill.  If s is the number of them <u>off sick</u>,
write an equation for the <u>number of directors</u> (D) at a meeting.

<u>ANSWER:</u>  It's number of directors = 1999 − number off sick.

So the answer is **D = 1999 − s.**

# Word Formulae and Equations

You can use equations for loads of other things, too — not just total cost.

## The Theme Park with a Difference

**EXAMPLE:** At Broughton Towers ("the Theme Park with a difference"), you pay a bargain £1 <u>entrance fee</u>, and <u>each ride</u> costs a pricy £196 once you're in.

If Glenn goes to Broughton Towers and goes on <u>R rides</u>, what will it cost him?

**ANSWER:** Glenn has to pay the bargain £1 entrance fee, and then £196 for each ride he goes on. That's £1 plus <u>£196 × the number of rides</u> he goes on. So the answer is $1 + 196 \times R$.

## Some Formulae are the Same

Watch out for this — some formulae that <u>look</u> different are really the <u>same</u>.

> It's like numbers. You know that 3, $1 + 2$ and $2 + 1$ are all the same, so if you have $1 + n$ and $n + 1$, they're the same too.

If someone came up to you in the street and offered to sell you the two numbers $2 \times 5$, and $5 + 5$, you would say "That's a con, they're the same number." Well, $2 \times n = n \times 2 = n + n$, too.

*Another trick that they like to sneak into your Tests is having <u>words</u> and <u>formulae</u> mixed up: "<u>one more than n</u>" and "$n + 1$" are the same.*

**EXAMPLE:** Match up the expressions that <u>mean the same</u> thing.

| | | |
|---|---|---|
| $n \times 1$ | $n$ | one less than n |
| n times itself | $n + n$ | $n - 1$ |
| | $n \times n$ | double n |
| $n^2$ | $2 \times n$ | |

**ANSWER:**
Basically, you need to <u>pick one</u>, see which others it's the <u>same</u> as, then move on to the next one. If you're not sure, you could always <u>try it</u> out with a few different numbers as n.

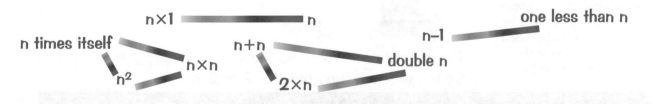

## No hedgehogs were harmed in the making of these pages

Our local grocer is doing a special offer on easy lemons (ideal for squeezing and mixing with peas for a tasty meal). If they cost 23p per lemon, and I buy n of them (I'm making lunch for some friends), what's the total cost T?

# Function Machines

When you put a number <u>into</u> a function machine it gives you a number <u>back out</u>. It has some kind of <u>rule</u> to get the new number from the one you give it — if you give it the same number lots of times it will <u>always</u> give the <u>same</u> answer.

**EXAMPLE:**  If I give this machine 3, it gives me 6.
If I give it 7, it gives me 14.
If I force it to take ½, it gives me 1.

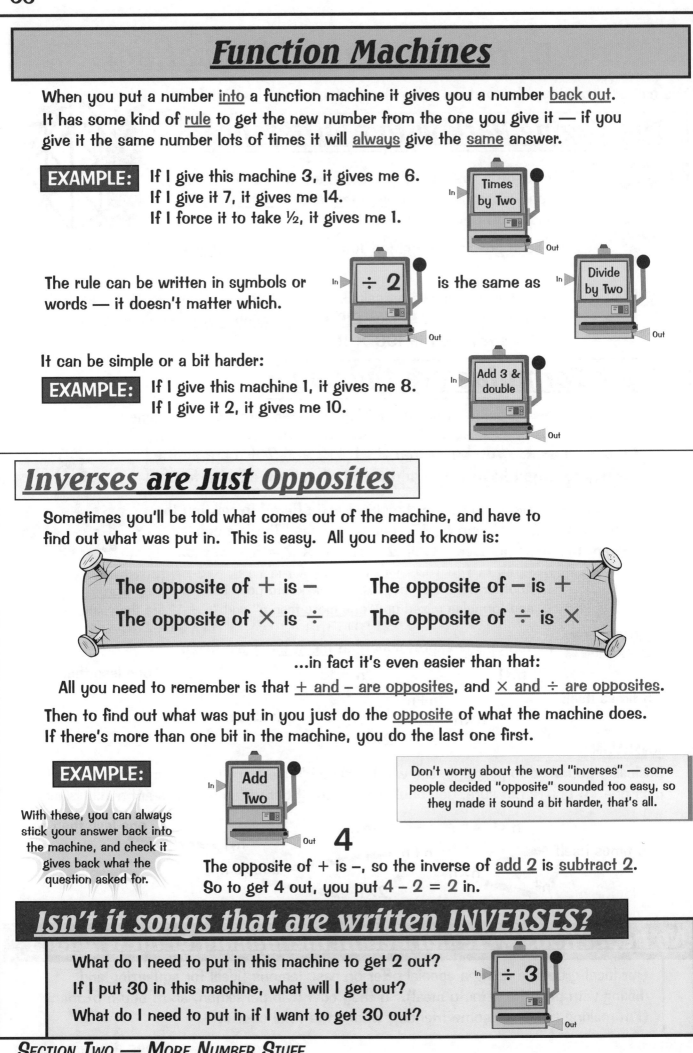

The rule can be written in symbols or words — it doesn't matter which.

In ÷ 2 Out   is the same as   In Divide by Two Out

It can be simple or a bit harder:

**EXAMPLE:**  If I give this machine 1, it gives me 8.
If I give it 2, it gives me 10.

In Add 3 & double Out

# Inverses <u>are Just Opposites</u>

Sometimes you'll be told what comes out of the machine, and have to find out what was put in.  This is easy.  All you need to know is:

| The opposite of + is −     The opposite of − is + |
| The opposite of × is ÷     The opposite of ÷ is × |

...in fact it's even easier than that:

All you need to remember is that <u>+ and − are opposites</u>, and <u>× and ÷ are opposites</u>.

Then to find out what was put in you just do the <u>opposite</u> of what the machine does. If there's more than one bit in the machine, you do the last one first.

**EXAMPLE:**

In Add Two Out  **4**

With these, you can always stick your answer back into the machine, and check it gives back what the question asked for.

Don't worry about the word "inverses" — some people decided "opposite" sounded too easy, so they made it sound a bit harder, that's all.

The opposite of + is −, so the inverse of <u>add 2</u> is <u>subtract 2</u>. So to get 4 out, you put 4 − 2 = 2 in.

# Isn't it songs that are written INVERSES?

What do I need to put in this machine to get 2 out?

If I put 30 in this machine, what will I get out?

What do I need to put in if I want to get 30 out?

In ÷ 3 Out

# Practice Questions

1) What's $\frac{2}{4}$ of 8?

2) Last night Tim baked his special "Rattlesnake Roll". The roll was 12 m long and Tim ate $\frac{3}{4}$ of it. What length of roll did Tim eat?

3) Which one of these is the same as $\frac{3}{6}$: $\frac{6}{12}$, $\frac{2}{6}$, $\frac{6}{3}$ or $\frac{2}{5}$?

4) Put these fractions in order of size, starting with the smallest: $\frac{1}{4}$, $\frac{3}{8}$, $\frac{1}{7}$, $1\frac{1}{2}$, $\frac{98}{99}$.

5) Answer the following, using fractions and decimals for the remainders
   a) $83 \div 4$      b) $48 \div 5$      c) $39 \div 6$

6) Convert these to fractions and decimals: 10%, 1%, 100%, 15%, 91%.

7) What's  a) 40% of 100?    b) 40% of 50?    c) 50% of 40?    d) 26% of 70?

8) This picture shows a design that Clarence is going to paint on a wall. Estimate:
   a) what fraction of the wall will be blue
   b) the percentage of the wall that will be yellow.

9) Larry has 4 red sheep, 6 blue sheep, and 5 green goats in his field.
   a) What is the ratio of red sheep to blue sheep in Larry's field?
   b) What proportion of the animals in the field are goats?

   *You'll probably need a calculator for question 11.*

10) Write out the first 10 multiples of 7.

11) Find all the factors of 28. Write them as factor pairs.

12) Write out 56 as a product of prime factors.

13) Pick out all the even, odd, prime and square numbers from this list:
    2, 3, 4, 5, 6, 7, 8, 9, 10

14) Look at this pattern: 1, 4, 7, 10, 13... What comes next? What's the 100th term?

15) What comes next in each of these patterns:
    a) 100, 99, 97, 94, 90...              b) 2, 6, 18, 54...
    c)

    ,              ,              ,              ...

16) Ace standard size cardboard boxes cost 9p each. If B is how many I buy, how much will it cost me, in pence?

17) A postal music company charges £100 postage and packing, and then £1 per CD. If Ruso buys C albums, how much will it cost her in total?

18) Here's a function machine: 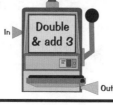 Double & add 3    In    Out
    a) If I give it 3, what do I get back?
    b) If I give it 0, what'll I get?
    c) What do I need to give it to get 7 back?

# Angles

## An Angle is a Measure of Turn

### What's an Angle?

The _angle_ between two lines is how much you have to _turn_ one of the lines so it matches up with the other one.

If you turn a line _all the way round_, then it will turn through an angle of 360° ("360 degrees").

No, I said an _angle_.

**EXAMPLE:** Below is a pair of lines. I can _turn_ one until they match up. The angle is _how much_ I've turned it. This time, it's ¼ of a full turn, or 90°.

The lines.

Here I've started turning one...

...and here I've finished. This amount of turn is 90°.

Watch out — the lines don't have to be the same length...

...and it doesn't matter which line you turn. You'll get the same answer.

---

Angles are given different _names_ according to how _big_ they are:

If it's less than a ¼ turn, then it's an **ACUTE** angle.

No, not a cute angle.

If it's exactly a ¼ turn, then it's a **RIGHT** angle.

If it's between a ¼ and ½ turn, then it's an **OBTUSE** angle.

If it's more than a ½ turn, then it's a **REFLEX** angle.

---

## You Can Use a Protractor to Measure Angles

45°

Made in Foxfield

If it's a reflex angle, then measure the one on the other side, and take it away from 360°.

Use this scale.

1) Put the cross on the protractor over the _corner_ of the angle you want to measure.
2) _Line up_ the bottom line of the protractor with one of the lines.
3) Find the scale of degrees that has 0 on the line of the angle.
4) Just _read off_ the angle.

# Angles

## Drawing Angles with a Protractor

1) Make sure your pencil is <u>really</u> sharp.
2) Use a ruler to draw a <u>straight</u> line, and put a <u>dot</u> at one end.
3) Put your protractor along this line, with its <u>cross</u> on the <u>dot</u>, and its <u>zero</u> on the line you've drawn.
4) Make a <u>mark</u> by the angle you want.
5) Draw a <u>straight</u> line from the end of your line to the mark. There you go, one angle, drawn to perfection.

## Estimate Angles by Comparing Them

If you want to know how <u>big</u> an angle is, but you haven't got a protractor, you can <u>estimate</u> it. The best way to do this is by <u>comparing</u> the angle you want to know with one of these special angles:

$\frac{1}{4}$ TURN
$90^0$

$\frac{1}{2}$ TURN
$180^0$

$270^0$
$\frac{3}{4}$ TURN

$360^0$
FULL TURN

You can try to see if your angle is a <u>bit more</u> or a <u>bit less</u> than one of these, and <u>add</u> a bit on, or <u>take</u> a bit off.

**EXAMPLES:**

This angle is just a little less than 90°. I'd estimate it's 80°.

This angle is a little bit less than 360°. If you ask me, I'd say it's 350°.

## Angles Stay the Same When You Scale Them

If you make a picture with an angle in it <u>bigger</u> or <u>smaller</u>, the angle <u>stays the same</u>.

**EXAMPLE:**

This angle is 90°.

And it's still 90°.

Aliens seen in Broughton  Daily Rubbish

## RIGHT angles? What about WRONG angles...

Estimate these angles, then measure them with a protractor. For each, say if it is an acute, obtuse or reflex angle.

1)    2)    3)    4)

5) Then draw these angles: 45°, 135°, and 315°.

# The Shapes You Need to Know

These are easy marks in the Test — Make sure you know them all!

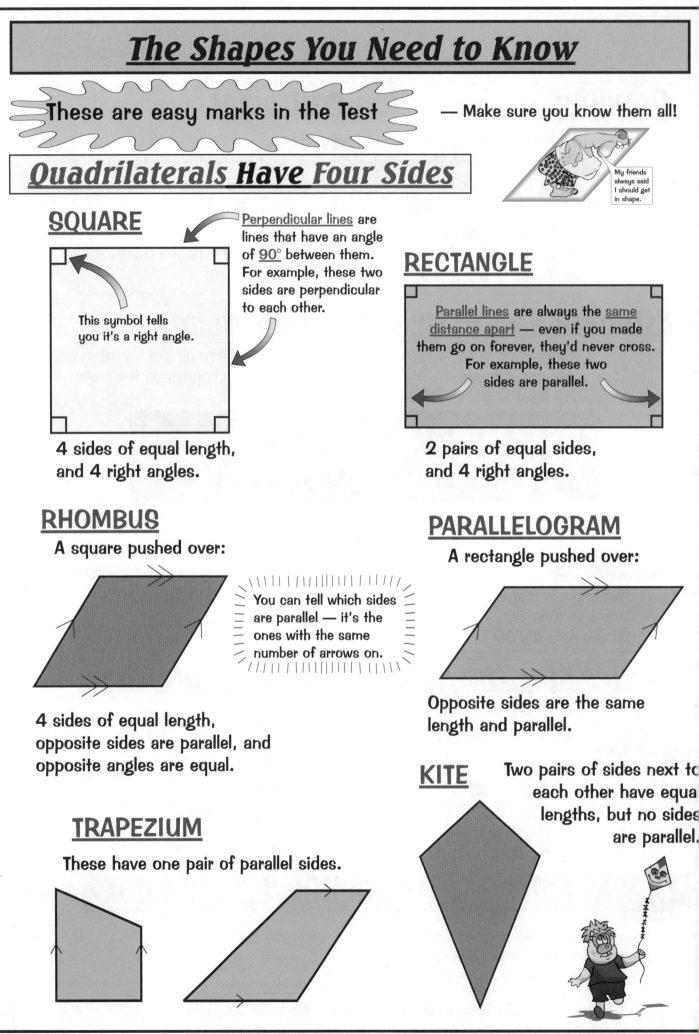

My friends always said I should get in shape.

## Quadrilaterals Have Four Sides

### SQUARE

Perpendicular lines are lines that have an angle of 90° between them. For example, these two sides are perpendicular to each other.

This symbol tells you it's a right angle.

4 sides of equal length, and 4 right angles.

### RECTANGLE

Parallel lines are always the same distance apart — even if you made them go on forever, they'd never cross. For example, these two sides are parallel.

2 pairs of equal sides, and 4 right angles.

### RHOMBUS

A square pushed over:

You can tell which sides are parallel — it's the ones with the same number of arrows on.

4 sides of equal length, opposite sides are parallel, and opposite angles are equal.

### PARALLELOGRAM

A rectangle pushed over:

Opposite sides are the same length and parallel.

### KITE

Two pairs of sides next to each other have equal lengths, but no sides are parallel.

### TRAPEZIUM

These have one pair of parallel sides.

# The Shapes You Need to Know

## There are Four Types of Triangle

### EQUILATERAL Triangle

3 sides of equal length,
3 equal angles.

60°
60°  60°

### SCALENE Triangle

All 3 sides different lengths.
All 3 angles different.

### RIGHT-ANGLED Triangle

One angle is a
right angle (90°).

### ISOSCELES Triangle

2 sides equal length,
and 2 angles equal.

The angles in a triangle
<u>always</u> add up to <u>180°</u>.

## Polygons Have Straight Sides...

...and the name tells you <u>how many</u> sides.

<u>Pentagons</u> have <u>five</u> sides,
<u>Hexagons</u> have <u>six</u> sides,
<u>Heptagons</u> have <u>seven</u> sides,
<u>Octagons</u> have <u>eight</u> sides...

Some hexagons.

It's not too hard to remember, "oct" sounds a little bit like
eight. Well, a <u>very little</u> bit. Hexagon is easy — <u>heXagon</u>
and <u>siX</u> both have an X in.

Remember, an octagon has eight SIDES,
it's an octopus that has eight LEGS.
Easy to get them mixed up, I know.

## Regular Polygons Have Equal Length Sides

### REGULAR PENTAGON

5 equal
sides.

### REGULAR HEXAGON

6 equal sides.

### REGULAR HEPTAGON

7 equal
sides.

A 50p piece is
a heptagon.

### REGULAR OCTAGON

8 equal sides.

EXIT
I'm off.

Not that kind of polygon.

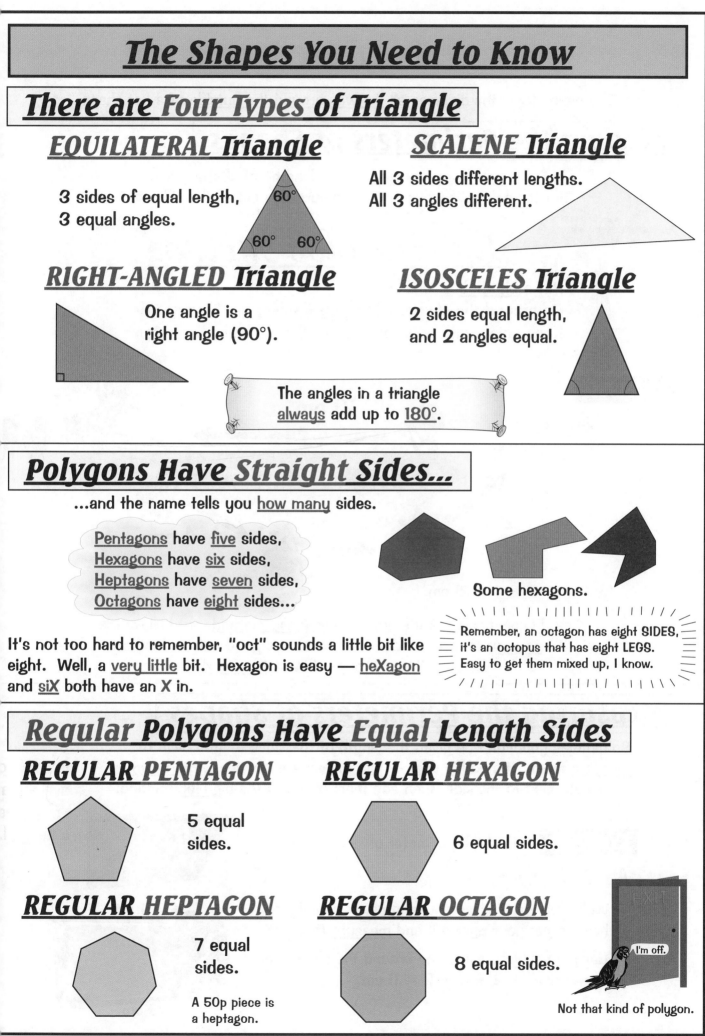

# Perimeters

The perimeter is the distance <u>all the way around the outside</u> of a flat shape.

## Finding the Perimeters of Shapes

To find a <u>perimeter</u>, you <u>add up</u> the lengths of all the sides,
but the <u>only reliable</u> way to make sure you get <u>all</u> the sides is this:

## The Big Blob Method

1) Put a <u>big blob</u> at one corner.
2) Go around the shape, <u>adding up</u> the length of every side.
3) Keep going until you get back to the big blob, then stop.

**EXAMPLE:**

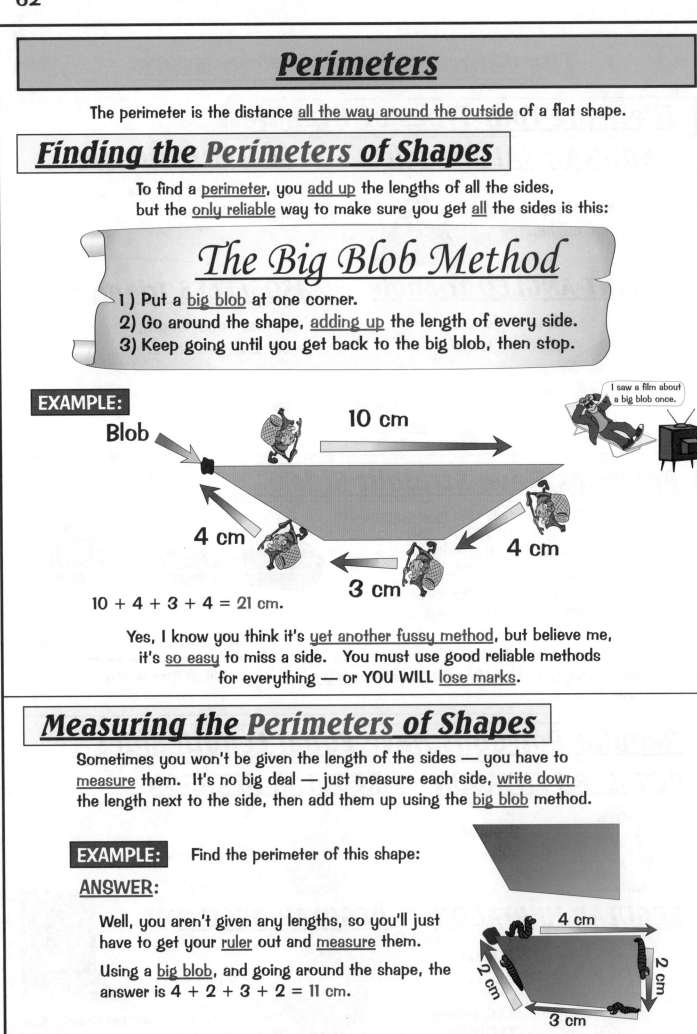

Blob

10 cm

4 cm

3 cm

4 cm

I saw a film about a big blob once.

10 + 4 + 3 + 4 = 21 cm.

Yes, I know you think it's <u>yet another fussy method</u>, but believe me,
it's <u>so easy</u> to miss a side.   You must use good reliable methods
for everything — or **YOU WILL** <u>lose marks</u>.

## Measuring the Perimeters of Shapes

Sometimes you won't be given the length of the sides — you have to
<u>measure</u> them.  It's no big deal — just measure each side, <u>write down</u>
the length next to the side, then add them up using the <u>big blob</u> method.

**EXAMPLE:**   Find the perimeter of this shape:

**ANSWER:**

Well, you aren't given any lengths, so you'll just
have to get your <u>ruler</u> out and <u>measure</u> them.

Using a <u>big blob</u>, and going around the shape, the
answer is 4 + 2 + 3 + 2 = 11 cm.

4 cm

2 cm

2 cm

3 cm

# Perimeters

If you are given <u>some</u> sides, but <u>not all</u> of them, you'll have to work the rest out.
Generally this is <u>really easy</u>, so don't panic.

## Working Out <u>Sides</u> You Don't Know

**EXAMPLE:** This is the desk from Katie the Giant's office.
What is its perimeter?

**ANSWER:** Well, we've been given the lengths of all the sides apart
from the <u>top one</u>, by her computer, but that side plus
2 m is the same as the one opposite, which is 4 m.
So it's fairly easy to work out that the top one is 2 m.

So putting a <u>big blob</u> on the corner, and
working around the shape, it's:
2+2+1+4+3+2 = 14 m.

> \\\\ | | | | | | | | | | | | | //
> Watch out... don't try to be too clever
> and measure the missing side.
> The drawing might not be quite right.
> Best work it out from what you're given.
> // / | | | | | | | | | | | | \\\\

**EXAMPLE:** You're in luck, I'm feeling generous, so I'll do one more.

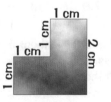

This shape has the <u>length</u> for one of the long
sides <u>missing</u>, but the two sides opposite it are
both 1 cm long, so <u>together</u> that makes 2 cm.

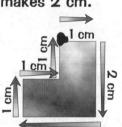

Write that in, draw a big blob on a corner, and add the numbers up.
It's 1+2+2+1+1+1 = 8. So the perimeter is 8 cm. Easy.

## Perim eaters love those tasty perims

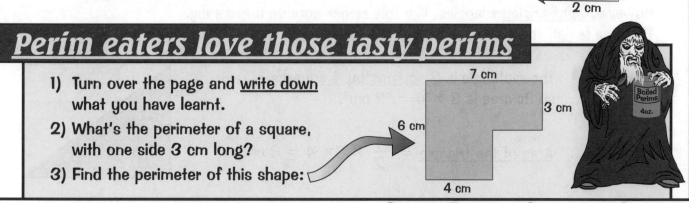

1) Turn over the page and <u>write down</u>
   what you have learnt.

2) What's the perimeter of a square,
   with one side 3 cm long?

3) Find the perimeter of this shape:

# Areas

Area can sound scary, but don't worry, it's just how much surface a shape covers.

## Finding the Area of Shapes by Counting

If a shape's on a <u>grid</u>, all you have to do to find its area is <u>count</u> how many <u>squares</u> it covers. You have to know how <u>big</u> each square is, too. Usually they'll have sides one centimetre long. Then you call them <u>square centimetres</u>, or <u>centimetres squared</u>. To save ink, time and effort, we write cm².

**EXAMPLE:** Find the area of this very boring purple rectangle.

*Sometimes the shape might not have squares in it, so you'll have to <u>draw your own</u> in. Make sure each of your squares is 1 cm².*

1 cm

<u>ANSWER:</u> There are <u>6 squares</u>, so the area is going to be 6. 6 what, though? Well, each square has sides 1 cm long, so they're <u>square centimetres</u>. So the answer is 6 square centimetres, or 6 cm².

## Rectangles — Just Multiply

With a rectangle, to get around the hassle of counting all the squares, you can use your <u>times tables</u> — just count how many squares there are <u>across</u> the rectangle, and how many there are <u>upwards</u>. Then <u>multiply</u> them together, and you've done it.

**EXAMPLE:** Work out the area of this slightly more interesting rectangle.

1 cm

<u>ANSWER:</u>

There are 3 LOTS OF 6 square centimetres in this rectangle. So the area is just $3 \times 6 = 18$ cm².

*If you think about it, when you're doing this, you don't even need to draw in all the squares. You could just measure each side and multiply them together.*

## A Triangle is Half of a Rectangle

<u>Counting</u> squares isn't very good for triangles because some squares are only part covered. However, <u>right-angled</u> triangles, like this rather cool one, are easy. The area is <u>half</u> the area of the rectangle the triangle is in.

1 cm

**EXAMPLE:** The rectangle is <u>3 squares</u> by <u>4 squares</u>, so its area is $3 \times 4 = 12$ cm².

So... <u>Area of the triangle</u> $= \frac{1}{2} \times 3 \times 4 = 6$ cm².

# Areas

## Building Up Big Shapes from Smaller Shapes

Sometimes you'll have to work out the area of a shape that's made up of <u>different</u> shapes <u>stuck together</u>. All you need to do is work out the areas for <u>each bit</u> and then <u>add them up</u>.

**EXAMPLE:** The <u>big square</u> has area $2 \times 2 = 4$ cm². The <u>small square</u> has area 1 cm². So the <u>total</u> area is $4 + 1 = 5$ cm². No problems.

**EXAMPLE:** Work out the area of this beautifully shaded shape.

<u>ANSWER:</u> The main thing is to <u>separate</u> it into the bits you can work out. There's a <u>rectangle</u> on the left, 3 squares high, and 2 wide, and a 3 by 4 <u>triangle</u> on the right.

Area of the rectangle: $3 \times 2 = 6$ cm².

Area of the triangle: $\frac{1}{2} \times 3 \times 4 = 6$ cm².

So the total area is $6 + 6 = 12$ cm².

## For Other Shapes, You Have to Count Squares

So what about circles, pentagons and hexagons? Or <u>real life</u> shapes like alien handprints, yeti footprints, or even leaves? You can get an estimate by <u>counting squares</u>. You count the squares that are <u>more than half</u> covered.

**EXAMPLES:**

Only the <u>four</u> squares with <u>ticks</u> in are more than half covered by this boring blue blob, so the area is near enough 4 cm². 1 cm

This footprint left by a lesser spotted Cumbrian Yeti has <u>two</u> squares that it <u>more than half</u> covers. So its area is about 2 cm².

## Shape up — it's not that bad...

<u>Memorise</u> the rules for finding the area of a shape. Then find the areas of these shapes:

1) 3 cm, 5 cm
2) 2 cm, 3 cm
3) 2 cm, 2 cm, 2 cm, 5 cm
4)

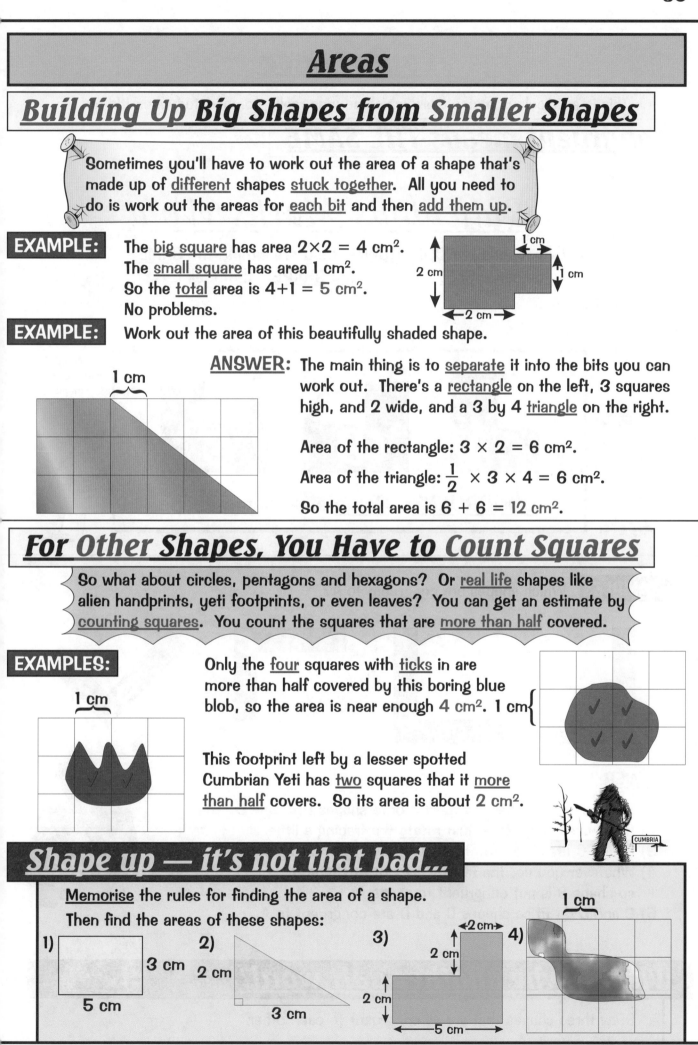

# Congruence

This is a ridiculous maths word which sounds really complicated when it's not:

## Congruent means THE SAME

### A Ridiculous Maths Word

If two shapes are CONGRUENT, they are simply the SAME
— the same SIZE and the same SHAPE. That's all it is.

% ^ M$%M
W$%M$E O$%
M"£~£"?

About
half past four
mate!

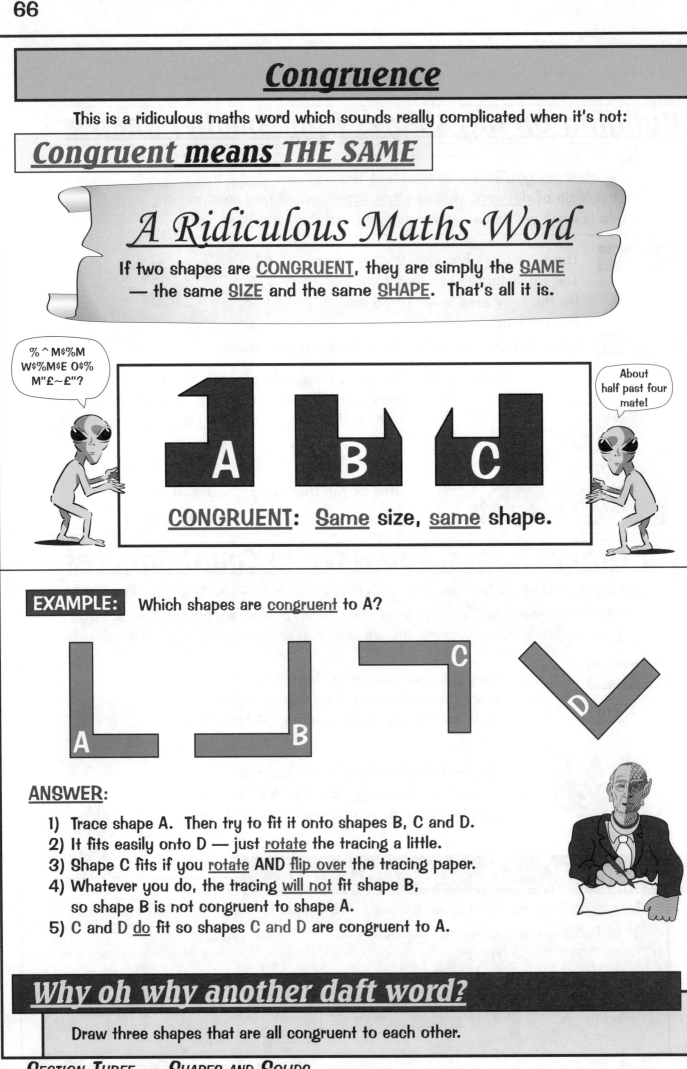

CONGRUENT: Same size, same shape.

---

**EXAMPLE:** Which shapes are congruent to A?

### ANSWER:

1) Trace shape A. Then try to fit it onto shapes B, C and D.
2) It fits easily onto D — just rotate the tracing a little.
3) Shape C fits if you rotate AND flip over the tracing paper.
4) Whatever you do, the tracing will not fit shape B,
   so shape B is not congruent to shape A.
5) C and D do fit so shapes C and D are congruent to A.

## Why oh why another daft word?

Draw three shapes that are all congruent to each other.

# Symmetry

Symmetry is all about <u>changing</u> a shape in some way
so that it still looks <u>exactly the same</u> as it did before.

## Line Symmetry Means Reflection

<u>Line symmetry</u> is where you can draw a <u>mirror line</u> (or more than one) so that
if you put a mirror along it, the shape looks the <u>same</u> as without the mirror.
The mirror line is also called the <u>line of symmetry</u>.

mirror

If you can draw <u>two</u> mirror lines you say there are <u>two</u>
lines of symmetry. If you can draw <u>three</u>, you say
there are <u>three</u> lines of symmetry, and so on. If you
can't draw <u>any</u>, then there are <u>no</u> lines of symmetry.

Simple enough: the number of lines
of symmetry is just the number of
places you can put a mirror without
changing how the shape looks.

| 1 LINE OF SYMMETRY | 2 LINES OF SYMMETRY | NO LINES OF SYMMETRY | 1 LINE OF SYMMETRY | 3 LINES OF SYMMETRY | NO LINES OF SYMMETRY |

## You Can Also Use Tracing Paper

If you <u>don't have</u> a mirror, you can use <u>tracing paper</u> instead. Trace the
shape, then to find out if a line is a line of symmetry, <u>fold</u> the paper
along it. If both sides <u>fit together</u> exactly, then it's a <u>line of symmetry</u>.

## Finding Lines of Symmetry

Basically there are <u>two</u> ways of doing this:

1) You can try to <u>guess</u>, and then <u>fold</u> the paper and see if you're right.

2) You can <u>bend</u> the paper over, and <u>turn it</u> until you can see a mirror line.

After a while you'll be able to <u>spot</u> lines of symmetry
<u>without</u> doing either of these, and that's the <u>best</u> way of all.

# Symmetry

## Rotational Symmetry is Just Turning

ROTATIONAL SYMMETRY is where you can _rotate_ the shape or drawing into different positions that all look _exactly_ the same.

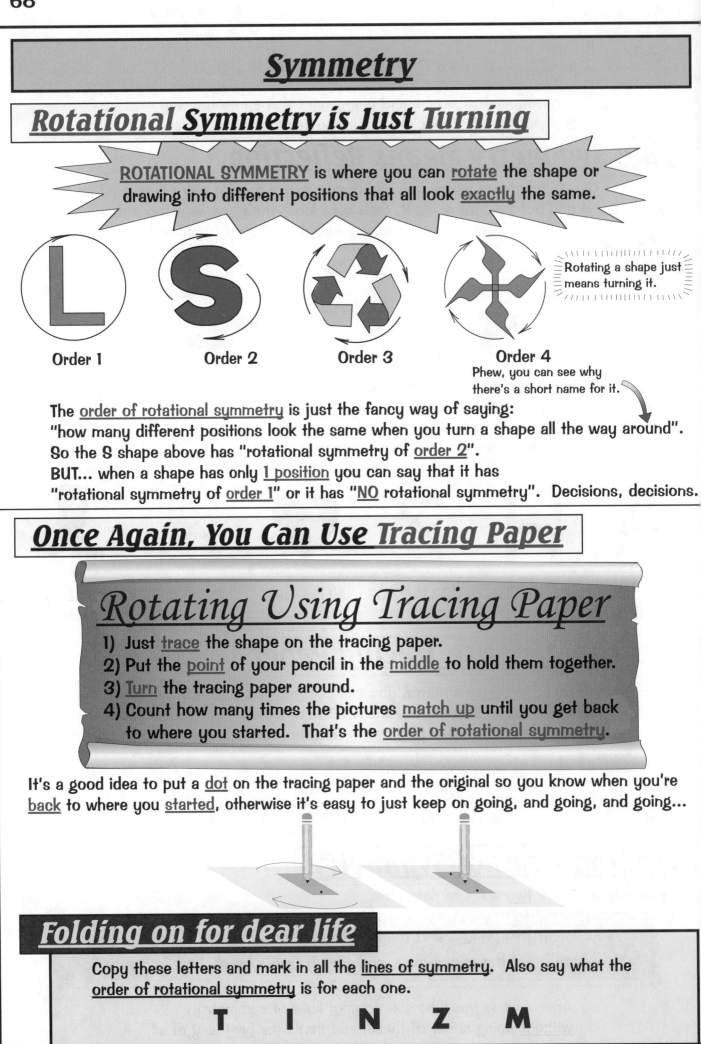

Order 1

Order 2

Order 3

Order 4

Rotating a shape just means turning it.

Phew, you can see why there's a short name for it.

The _order of rotational symmetry_ is just the fancy way of saying: "how many different positions look the same when you turn a shape all the way around". So the S shape above has "rotational symmetry of _order 2_". BUT... when a shape has only _1 position_ you can say that it has "rotational symmetry of _order 1_" or it has "_NO_ rotational symmetry".  Decisions, decisions.

## Once Again, You Can Use Tracing Paper

### Rotating Using Tracing Paper

1) Just _trace_ the shape on the tracing paper.
2) Put the _point_ of your pencil in the _middle_ to hold them together.
3) _Turn_ the tracing paper around.
4) Count how many times the pictures _match up_ until you get back to where you started.  That's the _order of rotational symmetry_.

It's a good idea to put a _dot_ on the tracing paper and the original so you know when you're _back_ to where you _started_, otherwise it's easy to just keep on going, and going, and going...

## Folding on for dear life

Copy these letters and mark in all the _lines of symmetry_.  Also say what the order of rotational symmetry is for each one.

# T  I  N  Z  M

# Reflection, Translation and Rotation

## Reflection in a Line

Shapes can be reflected <u>in a line</u>. We call it the <u>mirror line</u> because the <u>image</u>
you want is just what you'd see if you stuck a mirror on the paper along the line.

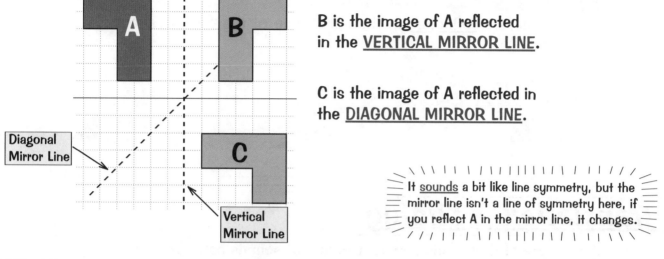

B is the image of A reflected
in the <u>VERTICAL MIRROR LINE</u>.

C is the image of A reflected in
the <u>DIAGONAL MIRROR LINE</u>.

It <u>sounds</u> a bit like line symmetry, but the
mirror line isn't a line of symmetry here, if
you reflect A in the mirror line, it changes.

---

The best way to <u>draw</u> the reflection of a shape in a line is using a mirror:

## Reflecting Shapes

1) Put a mirror upright on the mirror line so
that you can see the shape's <u>reflection</u>.

2) Look in the mirror and mark each corner
point of the image on the other side of
the line <u>where it appears to be</u>.

3) Join up the points to make the image.

4) <u>Check</u> that the reflection in the mirror is
the same as what you've drawn.

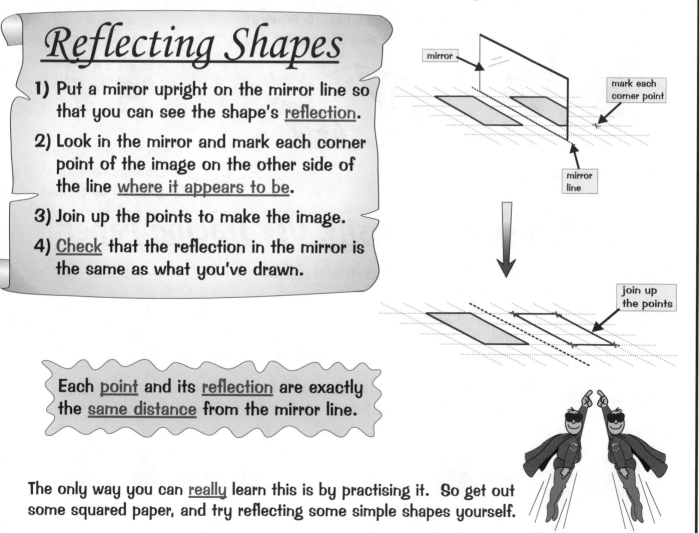

Each <u>point</u> and its <u>reflection</u> are exactly
the <u>same distance</u> from the mirror line.

The only way you can <u>really</u> learn this is by practising it. So get out
some squared paper, and try reflecting some simple shapes yourself.

# Reflection, Translation and Rotation

Yet again, you can use tracing paper to help, in case you don't have a mirror handy.

## Reflections Using Tracing Paper

1) Trace the shape and the mirror line onto the tracing paper.
2) Fold the paper over, along the mirror line.
3) You now have a reflection in the mirror line of the original shape.

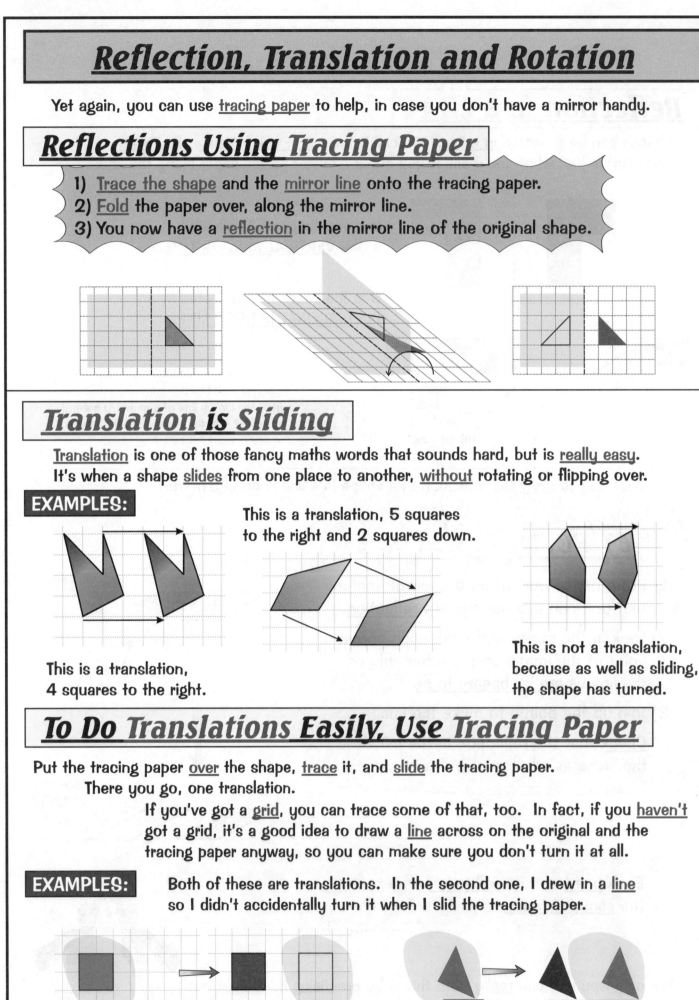

## Translation is Sliding

Translation is one of those fancy maths words that sounds hard, but is really easy. It's when a shape slides from one place to another, without rotating or flipping over.

**EXAMPLES:**

This is a translation, 5 squares to the right and 2 squares down.

This is a translation, 4 squares to the right.

This is not a translation, because as well as sliding, the shape has turned.

## To Do Translations Easily, Use Tracing Paper

Put the tracing paper over the shape, trace it, and slide the tracing paper. There you go, one translation.

If you've got a grid, you can trace some of that, too. In fact, if you haven't got a grid, it's a good idea to draw a line across on the original and the tracing paper anyway, so you can make sure you don't turn it at all.

**EXAMPLES:** Both of these are translations. In the second one, I drew in a line so I didn't accidentally turn it when I slid the tracing paper.

# Reflection, Translation and Rotation

## Rotating a Shape About a Point

Shapes can be rotated clockwise or anticlockwise <u>about a point</u>, called the <u>centre of rotation</u>. It is so easy, but if you forget about the centre of rotation, you'll lose out.

# Rotating Through 90° or 180°

1) Trace the shape <u>and</u> the point of rotation (the point you're rotating about).
2) Press a pencil on the <u>point of rotation</u> to hold the tracing paper in place.
3) **THE IMPORTANT BIT:** Look at one of the <u>horizontal</u> lines.
   a) <u>If it's a 90° turn</u>, turn the paper round until the line becomes vertical.
   b) <u>If it's a 180° turn</u>, turn the paper round until the line is horizontal again.
4) If there aren't any horizontal lines, use a vertical one and turn it to horizontal for <u>90°</u> or vertical for <u>180°</u>.

The distance of <u>any point</u> on the shape from the <u>rotation point</u> always <u>stays the same</u>.

Watch out — make sure you rotate in the right direction. Clockwise is the same way clock hands turn. Guess what... anticlockwise is the other way.

Clockwise: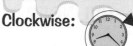

### EXAMPLE:

We get shape B by rotating shape A <u>anticlockwise</u> through 90° about point O.

Shape C is made by rotating shape A <u>through 180°</u> about point O.

If you're a bit confused by all this angle stuff, have a look at page 58.

Watch out, it really does make a difference where you rotate about. Try rotating triangle A about some other point to see it in action.

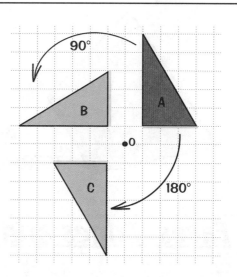

## Well there's plenty here for you to reflect upon...

1) Copy this diagram onto squared paper.
2) How can we get shape B from shape A?
3) Draw a <u>reflection</u> of A in the mirror line shown.
4) Draw shape B after it has been <u>translated</u> 7 squares to the left.

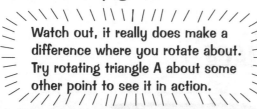

# 3-D Shapes You Need to Know

## You Need to Learn These Shapes

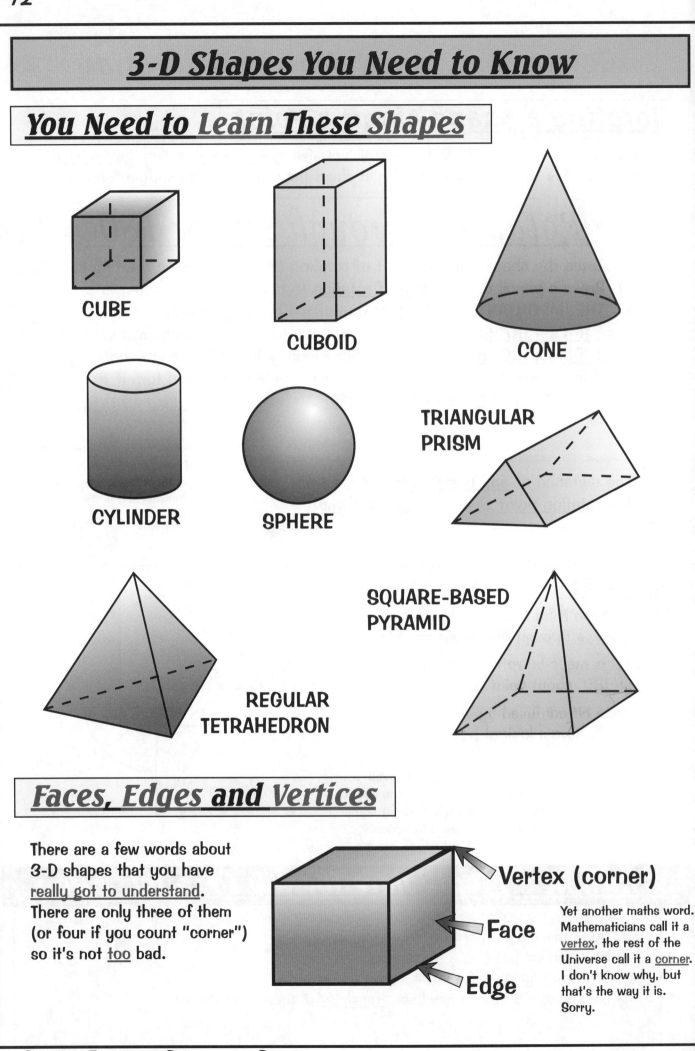

**CUBE**

**CUBOID**

**CONE**

**CYLINDER**

**SPHERE**

**TRIANGULAR PRISM**

**REGULAR TETRAHEDRON**

**SQUARE-BASED PYRAMID**

## Faces, Edges and Vertices

There are a few words about 3-D shapes that you have <u>really got to understand</u>. There are only three of them (or four if you count "corner") so it's not <u>too</u> bad.

**Vertex (corner)**

**Face**

**Edge**

Yet another maths word. Mathematicians call it a <u>vertex</u>, the rest of the Universe call it a <u>corner</u>. I don't know why, but that's the way it is. Sorry.

# Shape Nets

## A Shape Net Folds Up to Make a 3-D Shape

It's like this <u>cardboard box</u> I took apart. The flaps are there to glue it together with, so they weren't painted yellow after the box was made, like the outside of the box was. The <u>yellow</u> part is called the <u>net</u>.

## Shape Nets for Cubes

Just to add to the fun, there's <u>more than one net</u>. Here are a load of the different nets for cubes — don't panic, you don't have to know them all, as long as you don't fall into the <u>trap</u> of thinking there's only one.

Recognise this one?

Shape nets are ace...

# Shape Nets

## Some Other Shape Nets

Like I said before, you <u>don't</u> just have <u>one net</u> for each shape,
but I'll only show you one for each.

### 1) <u>Triangular Prism</u>

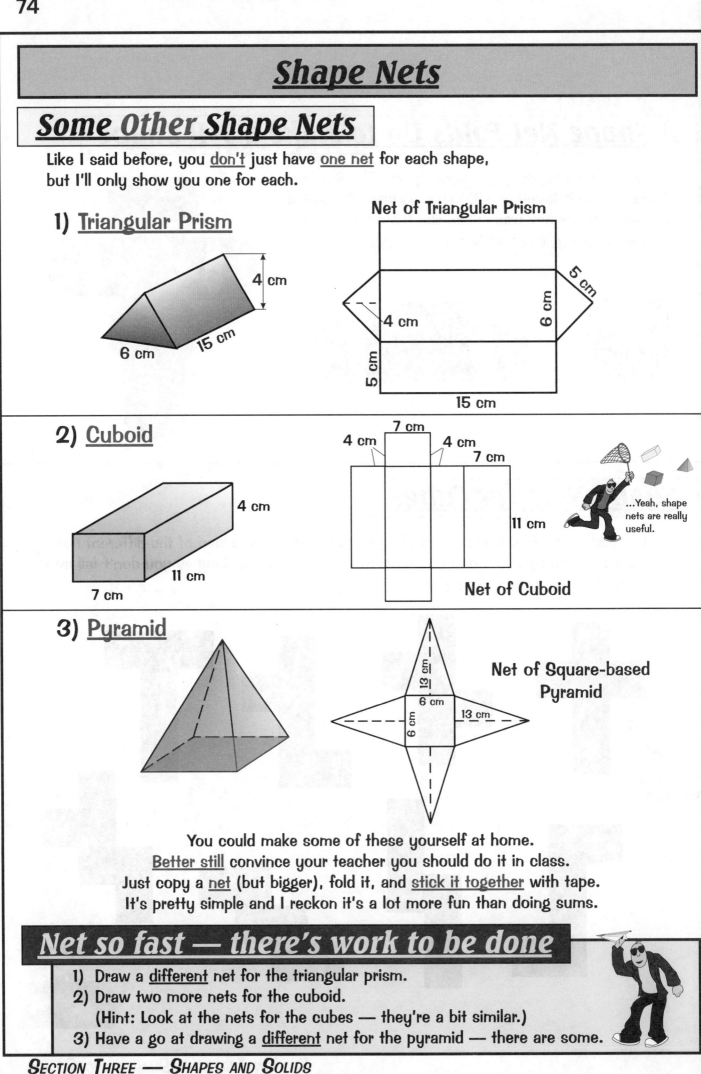

Net of Triangular Prism

4 cm

15 cm

6 cm

5 cm

4 cm

6 cm

5 cm

15 cm

### 2) <u>Cuboid</u>

4 cm

11 cm

7 cm

7 cm

4 cm    4 cm

7 cm

11 cm

Net of Cuboid

...Yeah, shape
nets are really
useful.

### 3) <u>Pyramid</u>

Net of Square-based
Pyramid

13 cm

6 cm

13 cm

6 cm

6 cm

You could make some of these yourself at home.
<u>Better still</u> convince your teacher you should do it in class.
Just copy a <u>net</u> (but bigger), fold it, and <u>stick it together</u> with tape.
It's pretty simple and I reckon it's a lot more fun than doing sums.

## Net so fast — there's work to be done

1) Draw a <u>different</u> net for the triangular prism.
2) Draw two more nets for the cuboid.
   (Hint: Look at the nets for the cubes — they're a bit similar.)
3) Have a go at drawing a <u>different</u> net for the pyramid — there are some.

# Practice Questions

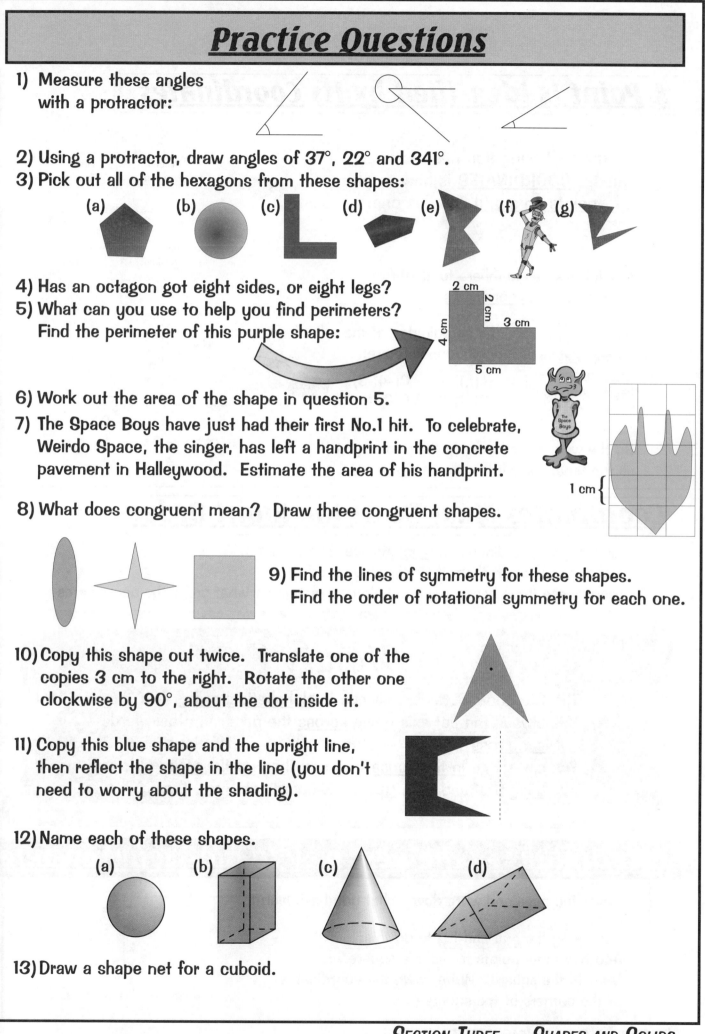

1) Measure these angles with a protractor:

2) Using a protractor, draw angles of 37°, 22° and 341°.

3) Pick out all of the hexagons from these shapes:

(a)  (b)  (c)  (d)  (e)  (f)  (g)

4) Has an octagon got eight sides, or eight legs?

5) What can you use to help you find perimeters?
Find the perimeter of this purple shape:

2 cm
2 cm
3 cm
4 cm
5 cm

6) Work out the area of the shape in question 5.

7) The Space Boys have just had their first No.1 hit. To celebrate, Weirdo Space, the singer, has left a handprint in the concrete pavement in Halleywood. Estimate the area of his handprint.

1 cm

8) What does congruent mean? Draw three congruent shapes.

9) Find the lines of symmetry for these shapes.
Find the order of rotational symmetry for each one.

10) Copy this shape out twice. Translate one of the copies 3 cm to the right. Rotate the other one clockwise by 90°, about the dot inside it.

11) Copy this blue shape and the upright line, then reflect the shape in the line (you don't need to worry about the shading).

12) Name each of these shapes.

(a)  (b)  (c)  (d)

13) Draw a shape net for a cuboid.

# Plotting Coordinates

## A Point Is Identified by Its Coordinates

The first thing you need to know about COORDINATES is how to plot points on a grid like this one.

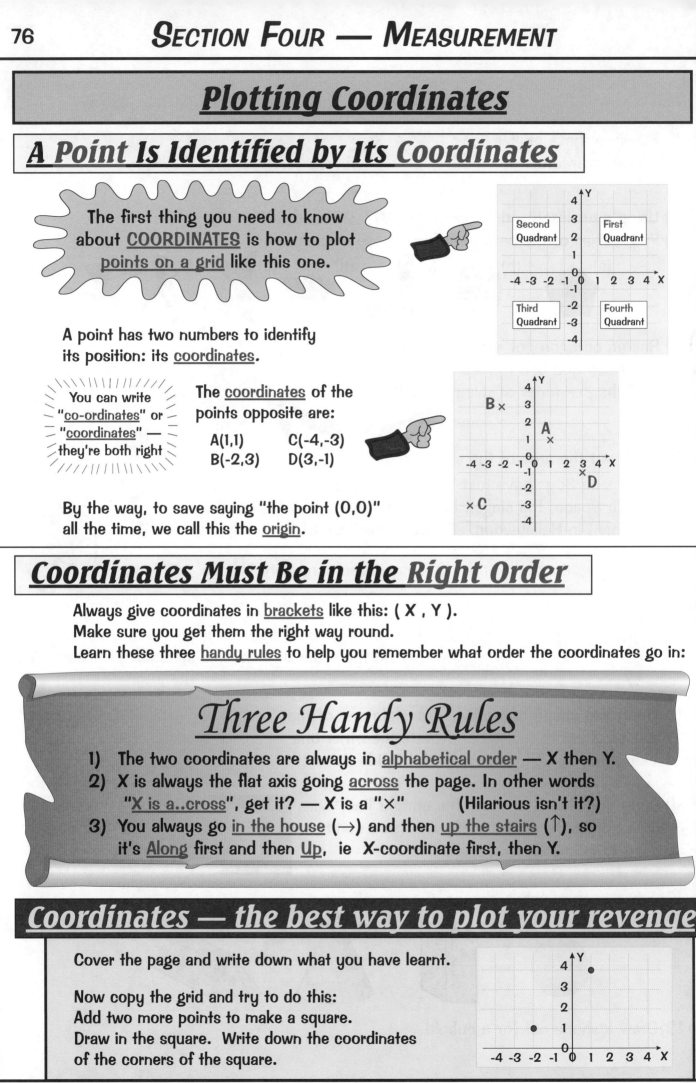

A point has two numbers to identify its position: its coordinates.

You can write "co-ordinates" or "coordinates" — they're both right

The coordinates of the points opposite are:

A(1,1)     C(-4,-3)
B(-2,3)     D(3,-1)

By the way, to save saying "the point (0,0)" all the time, we call this the origin.

## Coordinates Must Be in the Right Order

Always give coordinates in brackets like this: ( X , Y ).
Make sure you get them the right way round.
Learn these three handy rules to help you remember what order the coordinates go in:

# Three Handy Rules

1) The two coordinates are always in alphabetical order — X then Y.
2) X is always the flat axis going across the page. In other words "X is a..cross", get it? — X is a "×"     (Hilarious isn't it?)
3) You always go in the house (→) and then up the stairs (↑), so it's Along first and then Up, ie X-coordinate first, then Y.

## Coordinates — the best way to plot your revenge

Cover the page and write down what you have learnt.

Now copy the grid and try to do this:
Add two more points to make a square.
Draw in the square. Write down the coordinates of the corners of the square.

# Time

Here's a quick reminder about "<u>am</u>" and "<u>pm</u>" — though I'm sure you'll know it already:

"<u>am</u>" means "<u>Morning</u>" — it runs from 12 midnight to 12 noon.
"<u>pm</u>" means "<u>Afternoon and Evening</u>" — it runs from 12 noon to 12 midnight.

## The 24 Hour Clock Doesn't Stop at 12

If you've got a <u>video or DVD recorder</u> at home then you'll probably know the <u>24 hour clock</u> by now. But for those who haven't or don't, this is <u>what it's all about</u>:

$08:23:47$

$20:23:47$

The 24 hour time is the <u>same</u> as the 12 hour time if it's <u>morning</u> (except for the "<u>0</u>" at the front if it's before 10:00).

But you have to <u>add on 12 hours</u> if it's <u>afternoon</u>. So 20:23 is the same as **8:23 pm**.

When it gets to <u>midnight</u>, it goes from 23:59 to 00:00

## DON'T FORGET

1 day = 24 hours

1 hour = 60 minutes

1 minute = 60 seconds

## Calendars

What about them?
Hm-m-m... Let me think... These are really easy. You just have to <u>remember</u> that there are <u>12 months</u> OR <u>365 days</u> in <u>one year</u>. The weird bit is that there are 30 days in some months, 31 in others, and in February there are only 28! There's no way out — you'll just have to <u>learn</u> these:

Sometimes there are <u>29</u> days in February. This happens once every four years and is called a <u>leap year</u>.

"30 days has September,
April, June and November,
All the rest have 31,
Except February alone,
Which has 28 days clear,
And 29 in each leap year."

# Time

## Working Out Times

There's loads of stuff they can ask you about time, but the same GOOD OLD RELIABLE METHOD will work wonders for all of them.

### Remember

Take your time, write it down, and split it up

into SHORT EASY STAGES.

**EXAMPLE:** Conan the librarian starts stacking shelves at 7.45 am and finishes at 12.10 pm. How long does it take him?

**ANSWER:** What you don't do is try to work it all out in your head — this ridiculous method fails nearly every time. Instead, split it up into short easy stages:

7.45 ⟶ 8.00 ⟶ 12.00 ⟶ 12.10
15 mins     4 hours     10 mins

This is a nice safe way of finding the total time from 7.45 to 12.10:
4 hours + 15 mins + 10 mins = 4 hours 25 minutes.

## Who Is the Winner of the Race?

Maybe you think it's really complicated... But it isn't. Have a look yourself:

**EXAMPLE:** Three dogs are racing for the prize of a juicy bone. One of them finished the race in 2 minutes, another one in 1 minute and 45 seconds, and the other one finished in 1 minute. Who will get the bone?

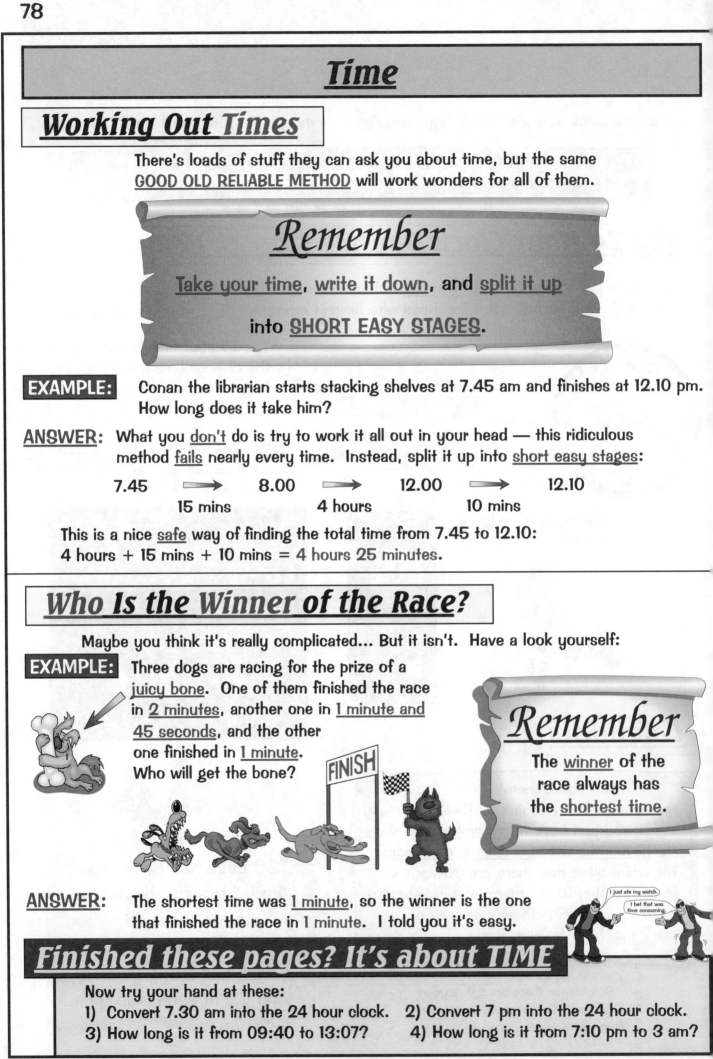

FINISH

### Remember

The winner of the race always has the shortest time.

**ANSWER:** The shortest time was 1 minute, so the winner is the one that finished the race in 1 minute. I told you it's easy.

*I just ate my watch.*
*I bet that was time consuming.*

## Finished these pages? It's about TIME

Now try your hand at these:
1) Convert 7.30 am into the 24 hour clock.    2) Convert 7 pm into the 24 hour clock.
3) How long is it from 09:40 to 13:07?      4) How long is it from 7:10 pm to 3 am?

*SECTION FOUR — MEASUREMENT*

# Timetables

## Reading Timetables

There is nothing scary about <u>timetables</u>.
In fact, you probably already know how to
read them, and haven't even realised!
Always <u>follow these easy steps</u>:

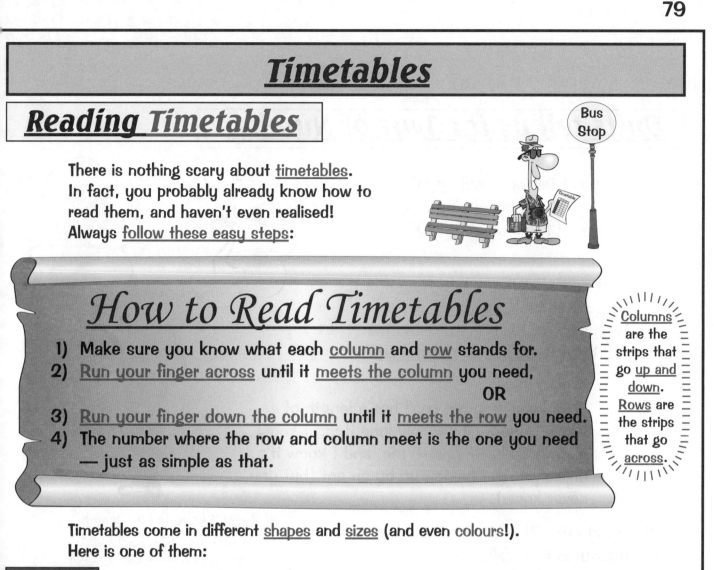

# How to Read Timetables

1) Make sure you know what each <u>column</u> and <u>row</u> stands for.
2) <u>Run your finger across</u> until it <u>meets the column</u> you need,
   OR
3) <u>Run your finger down the column</u> until it <u>meets the row</u> you need.
4) The number where the row and column meet is the one you need
   — just as simple as that.

<u>Columns</u> are the strips that go <u>up and down</u>. <u>Rows</u> are the strips that go <u>across</u>.

Timetables come in different <u>shapes</u> and <u>sizes</u> (and even colours!).
Here is one of them:

### EXAMPLE:

This tourist is taking an exciting train journey from
Millom to Barrow. At what time should he leave
Millom to be in Barrow by 3 o'clock?

<u>ANSWER</u>: Have a look at the timetable. You have to
remember that the times are in <u>24-hour clock time</u>.
Each column gives you the time for one train. This
means that there are <u>four trains a day</u>.

These are rows

| Millom | 1257 | 1428 | 1459 | 1623 |
| Green Road | 1302 | 1435 | 1503 | 1627 |
| Foxfield | 1305 | 1438 | 1507 | 1631 |
| Kirkby | 1309 | 1443 | 1511 | 1635 |
| Askam | 1314 | 1451 | 1516 | 1640 |
| Barrow | 1327 | 1459 | 1529 | 1653 |

These are columns

1) <u>Find</u> Barrow in the timetable.
2) <u>Follow that row</u> until the number in the column is the last one before 3 o'clock. It's 1459.
3) Then <u>follow up that column</u> until you reach the top row, which is the leaving time from Millom.

The final answer is 1428. This means that leaving at that time, our tourist will safely
arrive in Barrow by 3 o'clock to see the famous sandstone Town Hall.

# Units

## Units tell us the Type of Number

When you're talking about length, you can't just say something like, "my pet snail has a length of 10".

That doesn't tell you how long it is — it could be 10 centimetres, or 10 inches, or 10 miles, or even the length of 10 squashed cucumbers.

If you say "my pet snail has a length of 10 cm", then I know how long it is. I know it's not likely to squash me, and I know it's unlikely to get beaten up by an ant (but you never know).

The thing after 10 that tells you what it's measured in is called a unit.

It doesn't have to be a length. Just about anything you can measure has units — like volume, weight, time or temperature.

## Words like "Centi" tell you How Big a Unit is

You probably already know that there's 100 centimetres in a metre, but if you didn't know, you could work it out:

"Centi" means $\frac{1}{100}$ (one hundredth), so 1 centimetre is just $\frac{1}{100}$ of a metre. Here's some other useful words:

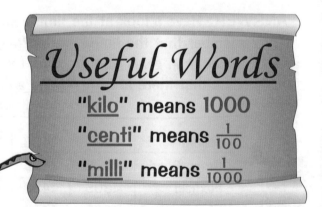

### Useful Words
"kilo" means 1000
"centi" means $\frac{1}{100}$
"milli" means $\frac{1}{1000}$

I'm 500 mm off the ground

**EXAMPLE:** How many millimetres are there in a metre?

**ANSWER:** "Milli" means $\frac{1}{1000}$, so there must be 1000 millimetres in a metre.

**EXAMPLE:** How many centilitres are there in a litre?

**ANSWER:** "Centi" means $\frac{1}{100}$, so there must be 100 centilitres in a litre.

# Units

It's a good idea to know <u>roughly how big</u> different units are.
Try to remember the examples on these pages, and think of others yourself.

## There's lots of different Length Units

I bet you already know how long a <u>centimetre</u> is.
If you've got a <u>ruler</u>, it will probably have centimetres
marked on it. The bits between the centimetres (cm)
are <u>millimetres</u> (mm) — there's <u>10</u> to each cm.

1 km is about $2\frac{1}{2}$ times around most athletics tracks, or a bit over half a mile.

1 inch

1 mm →

1 cm

A <u>kilometre</u> (km) is <u>1000 m</u> (remember from the last page that "<u>kilo</u>" means <u>1000</u>).

Your ruler will probably also have <u>inches</u>
marked. An inch is about $2\frac{1}{2}$ cm. If you
have a <u>30 cm ruler</u>, it will have <u>12 inches</u> on.
That's about the <u>height of this page</u>.

A foot is another name for 12 inches.

## Mass tells you How Heavy something is

A <u>kilogram</u> (kg) is <u>1000 grams</u> (g),
because "<u>kilo</u>" means <u>1000</u>.

Sugar often comes in 1 kg bags.

A medium sized apple has a mass of around 150 g. A small apple would be about 100 g.

Most cars have a mass of a bit over 1 tonne. A tonne is 1000 kg.

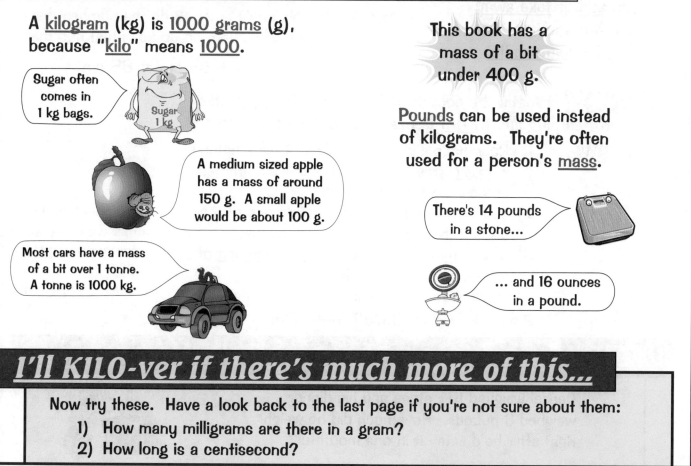

This book has a mass of a bit under 400 g.

<u>Pounds</u> can be used instead of kilograms. They're often used for a person's <u>mass</u>.

There's 14 pounds in a stone...

... and 16 ounces in a pound.

## I'll KILO-ver if there's much more of this...

Now try these. Have a look back to the last page if you're not sure about them:
1) How many milligrams are there in a gram?
2) How long is a centisecond?

# Units

## Volume is the Space something takes up

Liquids (like water or milk) have volume, which is just the amount of space something takes up.

Instead of cm³, people usually use millilitres (ml) for liquids, but they're both the same size. They might also say "capacity" instead of "volume"!

A tablespoon is 15 ml, and a teaspoon is 5 ml.

Volumes are sometimes measured in pints, especially for milk and other drinks.

A pint is a bit over $\frac{1}{2}$ a litre.

Large cartons of fruit juice are usually 1 litre.

PUREST SPRUCE JUICE

A litre is 1000 millilitres (because "milli" means $\frac{1}{1000}$).

## Adding and Subtracting Units

If a number has units after it, then you can only add or take away another number that has the same units.

**EXAMPLE:** What's the combined length of a 20 cm pickled turnip and a matching 65 cm aqualung?

**ANSWER:** This one's easy. Both the numbers have the same unit, so you can just add them:

20 cm + 65 cm = 85 cm.

**EXAMPLE:** What's the combined length of a 9 mm grated carrot earplug and a 17 m freeze-dried combine harvester?

**ANSWER:**
1) Now that's a bit harder. One of the lengths is in millimetres, but the other one's in metres, so you can't just add them.
2) You can only do it if you change one of them so that they both have the same units.
3) Now 9 mm is the same nine thousandths of a metre, so this is 0.009 m. If we write that instead, we can do the sum:

9 mm + 17 m = 0.009 m + 17 m = 17.009 m.

You could do it the other way around — just write 17 m as 17000 mm. Then the answer is 17009 mm.

## WEIGHT a minute — here's a question to do...

Denzel weighed $10\frac{1}{2}$ stone and his dinner weighed 8 pounds. How much did he weigh right after he'd eaten it in one mouthful?

# Conversions

## Conversion Factors

A <u>conversion factor</u> is just a number that you use to convert one thing to another, like <u>feet to metres</u>, or <u>grams to kilograms</u>. You either <u>multiply or divide</u> by it, depending on what you're converting. If you're not sure whether to multiply or divide, then do both and then pick the <u>common-sense answer</u>.

**EXAMPLE:** If 1 metre is equal to 3.28 feet, how many feet long is a 5 metre slug?

Step 1) Find the <u>conversion factor</u>: here the conversion factor is obviously <u>3.28</u>.

Step 2) <u>Multiply or divide</u> by the conversion factor, or do both if you're not sure:

$5 \times 3.28 = 16.4$
$5 \div 3.28 = 1.52...$

Step 3) Choose the <u>common-sense</u> answer: Not too obvious, but if 3 feet are about 1 metre, then 1.52 feet can't be anywhere near 5 metres, so the slug must be 16.4 feet long.

Make sure you know these <u>common conversion factors</u>:

1 <u>cm</u> = 10 mm

1 <u>m</u> = 100 cm

1 <u>km</u> = 1000 m

1 <u>tonne</u> = 1000 kg

1 <u>kg</u> = 1000 g

1 <u>litre</u> = 1000 ml

1 <u>metre</u> is a bit over 3 feet.
1 <u>kilogram</u> is a bit over 2 pounds.
2 pints are a bit over 1 <u>litre</u>.

**EXAMPLE:** A popular item at our local supplies is "Froggatt's Mashed Sprout Window Cleaner" (not available in all areas). The Farmhouse Economy Size is the most popular and weighs 1500 g. How much is this in kg?

Step 1) <u>Conversion Factor</u> = 1000 (simply because 1 kg = 1000 g)

Step 2) $1500 \times 1000 = 1\,500\,000$ kg (Uulp...)
$1500 \div 1000 = 1.5$ kg (That's more like it.)

Step 3) So the answer must be that 1500 g = 1.5 kg.

# Conversions

## Conversion Graphs

You probably don't believe this, but <u>conversion graphs</u> are really helpful. Usually graphs are a bit scary, but <u>these ones are OK</u>. You'll need them to convert <u>between</u> things like:

Pints ➡ Litres     Miles ➡ Kilometres

Feet ➡ Metres     Pounds ➡ Kilograms

Reading graphs is very easy. Just <u>remember</u> to follow these four simple steps:

## How to Read Graphs

1) <u>Draw a line</u> up from the value on the across axis.
2) Keep going until you <u>hit the line</u>.
3) Then <u>change direction</u> and go across to <u>the other axis</u>.
4) <u>Read off the new value</u> from the axis. <u>That's the answer</u>.

*You can also read it the other way round — draw a line <u>from</u> the upright axis, then <u>go down</u> when you hit the line.*

**EXAMPLE:** In the beauty competition "Miss WormWorld-99" the Princess of Worms was weighed. Her weight was exactly 8 pounds. How many kilograms is this?

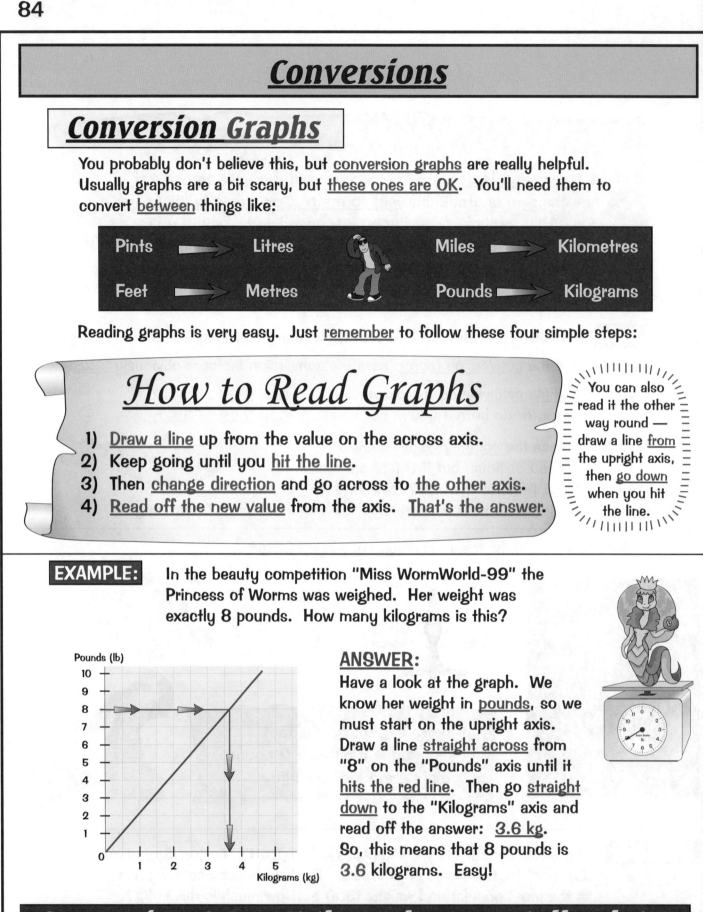

**ANSWER:**
Have a look at the graph. We know her weight in <u>pounds</u>, so we must start on the upright axis. Draw a line <u>straight across</u> from "8" on the "Pounds" axis until it <u>hits the red line</u>. Then go <u>straight down</u> to the "Kilograms" axis and read off the answer: <u>3.6 kg</u>. So, this means that 8 pounds is 3.6 kilograms. Easy!

## Conversions? Aren't they when you talk a lot...

Learn the conversions on these pages, then cover them up and write them down.

1) How many cm is a 3 metre hamster?    2) How many mm is a 4 cm purple donkey?
3) How many kg is a 1500 g carrot?      4) How many litres is a 2000 ml cup of tea?

# Reading Scales

You've probably got lots of scales lying around at home.  A scale is just something with lots of <u>lines and numbers</u> that you use to <u>measure things</u> — like <u>rulers</u>, <u>kitchen scales</u>, <u>measuring jugs</u> and <u>thermometers</u>.
Reading scales is pretty simple — just follow these steps:

## How to Read Scales

1) If the thing you're measuring <u>lines up</u> with a number on the scale, then just <u>read off the number</u>.
2) Otherwise you'll have to work out how big the <u>divisions</u> of the scale are, and <u>count</u> the number of divisions.
3) When you give your answer, always say whether it's in <u>metres</u> or <u>centimetres</u> or whatever.

**EXAMPLE:**

After 120 years of dieting, Drago decided to weigh himself.  What was his weight?

<u>ANSWER:</u>

You don't even have to think about this one!  Just look carefully at the picture — the arrow on the scales is showing exactly <u>240</u>!  Just make sure you <u>know what this 240 stands for</u> (in this case it's <u>kilograms</u>).
So Drago's weight was 240 kg.

It's all those curries...

... and late nights...

I'm starving...

For scales the <u>number line</u> comes in handy.
The number line is a <u>very long line</u> (in fact it goes on forever, but the page isn't quite long enough).

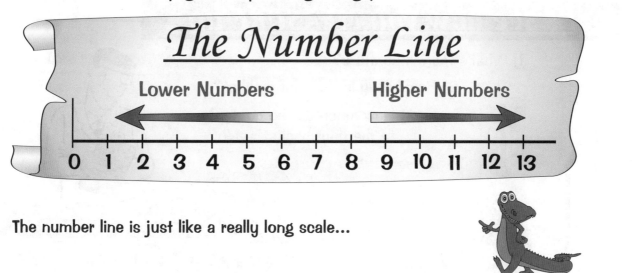

## The Number Line

Lower Numbers      Higher Numbers

0  1  2  3  4  5  6  7  8  9  10  11  12  13

The number line is just like a really long scale...

# Reading Scales

## Measuring Things with a Ruler

If you have a look at the ruler, you'll find that it looks nearly the same as the number line.

**EXAMPLE:** How tall is Dolly the bulldog?

I'm a RULER!

ANSWER: All you have to do is:

Step 1) Try to stand Dolly <u>still</u> next to the ruler. (Don't worry, she won't bite...)
Step 2) Draw an imaginary line <u>from</u> the top of her head <u>towards</u> the ruler.
Step 3) Take a <u>reading</u>. 70 cm is the answer.

I think it's gone off

**EXAMPLE:** How much 3-year-old milk does this beaker contain?

**ANSWER:** This one's easy. The level of liquid lines up exactly with the 900 ml line, so the amount of milk is 900 ml.

**EXAMPLE:**

How much slime is there in this measuring cylinder?

ANSWER: This one's a bit harder, so I'll break it into the three steps:

Step 1) Look at the scale. The level of slime is <u>between 40 and 50 ml</u>, so you can't just read off a number.

Step 2) There are <u>four lines</u> on the scale between 40 and 50 — that means it's divided into <u>five</u> bits. 40 ml to 50 ml is <u>10 ml</u>, so each bit must be <u>2 ml</u> (10÷5=2).

Step 3) The level goes up to the top of the <u>3rd</u> bit, so:

total = 40 ml + 3 bits = 40 + 6 ml = 46 ml.

So there's 46 ml of slime.

## Let's see how you MEASURE up...

1) What's the temperature?
2) How heavy is the zapf dingbat?
3) How much do the contents of the flour packet weigh?
4) How long is the alien?

# Maps and Compass Directions

## Map References Tell You Where You Are

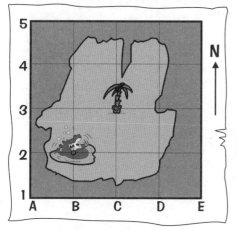

A map reference just tells you where something is on a map. They're just like coordinates, which are on page 30. The main difference is that a map sometimes has letters instead of numbers.

**EXAMPLE:**

This map shows the Land of the Killer Hippo. What are the map references of the Killer Hippo and its favourite tree, Boris?

**ANSWER:** We'll do the hippo first. There are three steps:

Step 1)  Start in the bottom left corner and read from left to right until you're below the hippo — that takes you to B.

Step 2)  Now just go up until you get to the hippo, and read off the number to the left — which is 2.

Step 3)  Combine the letter and the number to give you the map reference.

So the map reference of the Killer Hippo is B2, and by the same method Boris the tree is at C3.

## The Compass Has Eight Main Points

Make sure you know these eight compass directions. They're pretty useful for saying which way something's going.

**EXAMPLE:** On the map at the top of the page, the Killer Hippo is south-west of the tree. Or looked at another way, Boris is north-east of the Killer Hippo.

## Now for some PLAN-tastic questions...

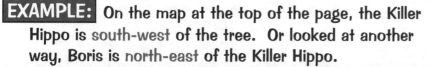

This map shows the route of Herman Bogden on his holiday in the Haggis Islands.

1) What is the map reference of the infamous Sumo Hamster?

2) Where did Mr Bogden leave his brain?

3) Where did his car get bogged down?

4) What direction would Mr Bogden have to go in to find his brain?

5) What direction would the Sumo Hamster have to go in to get there first?

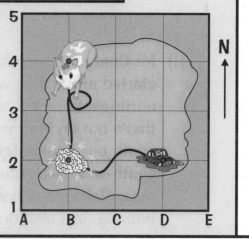

# Practice Questions

1) Copy the grid opposite, then plot the points A(1,1); B(1,4); C(3,2); D(5,4) and E(5,1). As you plot each point, join it with a straight line to the one before. Which letter can you see?

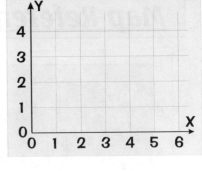

2) How many days are there in between 27th of April and 13th of May?

3) Betty the cow went for a swim at 9 am. It took her 330 minutes before she came back. What time did she get back home? Give your answer in both the 12 hour and the 24 hour clock.

| Uranus | 0910 | 1050 | 1230 |
|--------|------|------|------|
| Saturn | 0945 | 1125 | 1305 |
| Jupiter | 1010 | 1150 | 1330 |
| Mars | 1024 | 1204 | 1344 |
| Earth | 1059 | 1239 | 1324 |

4) Here is a piece of the timetable of the "Super Space Shopper Coach". At what time does Nure the alien have to leave Saturn to arrive on Mars by quarter to two?

5) a) What is the length, in centimetres, of a metre long worm?
   b) How many millimetres is it from my house to the grocers shop that is two kilometres away?

6) I drive a ten metre long bus, and when I go on holiday, I need a 60 centimetre long trailer to put my suitcases in. How long are the bus and trailer combined?

7) How many grams are in a 2.5 kg jar of pickled tadpoles?

9) How long is this elephant (including its trunk and tail)?

8) How many pounds (lb) is a 4 kilogram Green Siberian baboon?

10) What is the temperature of this lovely cup of tea?

11) Mr Chezwick went for a walk in the park. He started at B1, then walked north two squares, north-east one square (crossing over a river that's not on the map), east one square, south one square (going over the river again), south-west two squares. Make a copy of this map. Joining the lines, show Mr Chezwick's journey, and also draw the river.

*SECTION FOUR — MEASUREMENT*

# Tables

## Tables make things Easier to Read

This is a <u>table</u>.   The table shows some of Simon and Kate's favourite things.
Tables are <u>quicker to read</u> than long lists.

|  | Simon | Kate |
|---|---|---|
| Favourite Food | Blancmange on toast | Gerbil flavour sawdust |
| Favourite Drink | Liquefied cheesecake | Salted sprout juice |
| Favourite Sport | Unicycle sumo wrestling | Hippopotamus tickling |
| Favourite Pastime | Yodelling | Underwater Cluedo |

The words in the purple bits are the <u>headings</u>. You can use them to find out what's in the rest of the table.

**EXAMPLE:**   What is <u>Simon's favourite sport</u>?

**ANSWER:**

1) First look at the <u>headings</u>.  Find where it says "<u>Simon</u>" along the top, then find where it says "<u>Favourite Sport</u>" on the left hand side.

2) Now move one finger <u>down</u> from "Simon" and another <u>along</u> from "Favourite Sport".  Your fingers will meet at Simon's favourite sport, which is <u>unicycle sumo wrestling</u>.

Drawing <u>lines</u> can sometimes help you find something in a table.

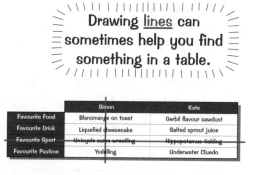

## Distance Tables only have One Lot of Headings

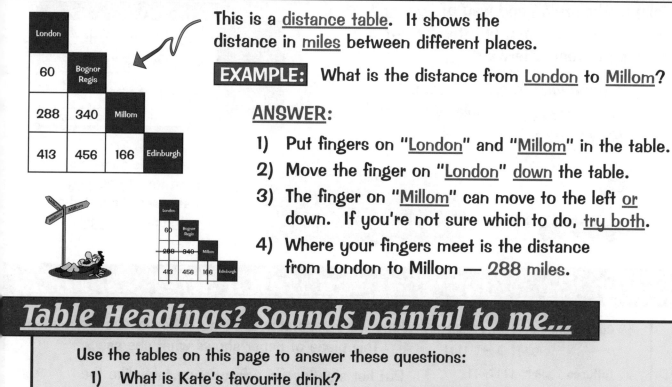

This is a <u>distance table</u>.  It shows the distance in <u>miles</u> between different places.

**EXAMPLE:**   What is the distance from <u>London</u> to <u>Millom</u>?

**ANSWER:**

1) Put fingers on "<u>London</u>" and "<u>Millom</u>" in the table.

2) Move the finger on "<u>London</u>" <u>down</u> the table.

3) The finger on "<u>Millom</u>" can move to the left <u>or</u> down.  If you're not sure which to do, <u>try both</u>.

4) Where your fingers meet is the distance from London to Millom — <u>288 miles</u>.

## Table Headings? Sounds painful to me...

Use the tables on this page to answer these questions:
1) What is Kate's favourite drink?
2) What is the distance from Bognor Regis to Millom?

# Tally Marks

## Tally Marks make sure you don't Lose Count

These are <u>tally marks</u>. They make sure you don't <u>lose count</u> when you're counting something.

They're good for counting things like laps in a race:

1) Each time someone does a lap, you add another mark.
2) After the race, you count them to find how many they've done.

|

||

|||

||||

This is 4

This is 5 ⟶ ||||

This is 6 ⟶ |||| |

Whenever you have <u>4</u> lines together, the next line always goes <u>across</u> it. That makes them easier to count.

**EXAMPLE:** Jeremiah decided to count the number of <u>points</u> scored by each player in a game of pogo-stick volleyball.

He wrote down the players' <u>names</u>, then drew a <u>tally mark</u> next to each player whenever they <u>scored</u> a point.

Bob || 

Sue |||| 

Zebedee |||| |||| |||| ||| 

Gawain ||| 

Hercules |||| ||| 

Pete |||| 

## Frequency Tables show the Tally Totals

Tally marks are a good way of <u>counting</u> the scores in a game, but they're not so easy to read afterwards.

A good way to show them is with a <u>frequency table</u>, which shows the <u>totals</u> as well.

|  | Tally | Total Score |
|---|---|---|
| Bob | || | 2 |
| Sue | |||| | 5 |
| Zebedee | |||| |||| |||| ||| | 18 |
| Gawain | ||| | 3 |
| Hercules | |||| ||| | 8 |
| Pete | |||| | 5 |

The numbers or words in a table or list are sometimes called "<u>data</u>".

The total is sometimes called the "<u>frequency</u>". That's why it's called a "<u>frequency table</u>".

## Tally? Isn't that what you watch after school...

Cucumbers |||| |||| |||| 
|||| |||| ||||

Lettuces |||| |||| ||

Giraffe-infested carrots |||

June went vegetable spotting in her local supermarket. ⟵ This piece of paper shows what she saw.

Put her sightings in a frequency table like the one above, showing the tally marks and totals.

# Bar Charts

## Bar Charts show things at a Glance

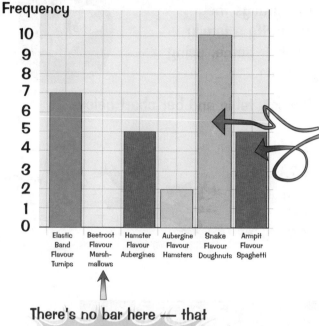

Frequency

⟵ This is a bar chart.
It shows the sales of 6 top
Froggatt's products in one
day from our local store.

These coloured bits going up the
chart are called "bars" — that's
why it's called a "bar chart".

The heights of the bars just tell you
how many of each product were sold.

There's no bar here — that
means that no beetroot
flavour marshmallows were
sold. I can't think why.

Bar charts make life easy
— you can compare
things without looking at
lots of numbers.

---

**EXAMPLE:** According to the bar chart, how
many snake flavour doughnuts were sold?

ANSWER:

1) First look along the bottom of the chart
until you find "Snake Flavour Doughnuts".
2) Now look at the bar above it.
3) What you want is the number to the left
that lines up with the top of the bar.
In this case, it's 10, so 10 snake flavour
doughnuts were sold.

You're a snake
I'm knot!

A ruler might help
you to see which
number lines up with
the top of the bar.

## Bar Charts can be drawn Sideways Too

Bar charts can sometimes
be drawn sideways as well.
Here's what the one above
looks like on its side.

Elastic Band Flavour Turnips

Beetroot Flavour Marshmallows

Hamster Flavour Aubergines

Aubergine Flavour Hamsters

Snake Flavour Doughnuts

Armpit Flavour Spaghetti

0 1 2 3 4 5 6 7 8 9 10
Frequency

You read them the same way — except
you start at the side and look down!

# Bar Charts

## Drawing a Bar Chart isn't Scary

**EXAMPLE:**

25 ghosts were asked how many days they thought it would take them to terrify a family (including any animals) out of their home, using only a sheet and woooooing noises.

Their answers are shown in the list, table and bar chart below.

Always <u>cross out</u> numbers as you tally them up. That makes sure you don't forget any numbers, or do them twice.

13, 51, 3, 5, 17,
25, 32, 43, 67, 24,
33, 29, 20, 55, 25,
35, 12, 28, 48, 23,
27, 59, 65, 82, 90

| Days | Tally | Frequency |
|---|---|---|
| 0 to 20 | ⦀⦀ \| | 6 |
| 21 to 40 | ⦀⦀ ⦀⦀ | 10 |
| 41 to 60 | ⦀⦀ | 5 |
| 61 to 80 | \|\| | 2 |
| 81 to 100 | \|\| | 2 |

The first thing you have to do is write on these numbers, making sure that all the bars will fit on the chart.

The numbers don't always go up in ones. If the bars were very big, it might go 0, 100, 200, 300...

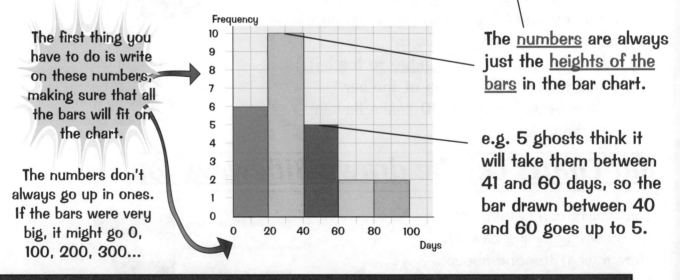

The <u>numbers</u> are always just the <u>heights of the bars</u> in the bar chart.

e.g. 5 ghosts think it will take them between 41 and 60 days, so the bar drawn between 40 and 60 goes up to 5.

## Bar Charts — and the new number one is...

Look again at the bar charts on the last page.
1) How many hamster flavour aubergines were sold?
2) How many elastic band flavour turnips were sold?

# Pictograms

## Pictograms are Numbers in Pictures

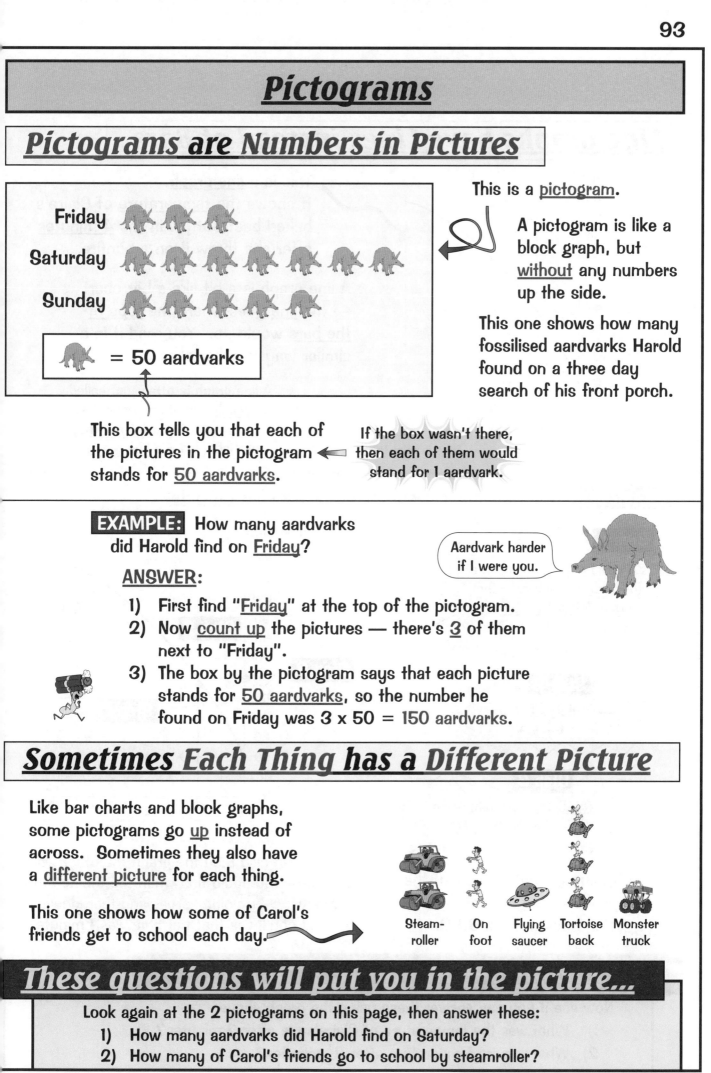

Friday 🦫 🦫 🦫

Saturday 🦫 🦫 🦫 🦫 🦫 🦫 🦫

Sunday 🦫 🦫 🦫 🦫 🦫

🦫 = 50 aardvarks

This is a pictogram.

A pictogram is like a block graph, but without any numbers up the side.

This one shows how many fossilised aardvarks Harold found on a three day search of his front porch.

This box tells you that each of the pictures in the pictogram stands for 50 aardvarks.

If the box wasn't there, then each of them would stand for 1 aardvark.

**EXAMPLE:** How many aardvarks did Harold find on Friday?

Aardvark harder if I were you.

**ANSWER:**

1) First find "Friday" at the top of the pictogram.
2) Now count up the pictures — there's 3 of them next to "Friday".
3) The box by the pictogram says that each picture stands for 50 aardvarks, so the number he found on Friday was 3 x 50 = 150 aardvarks.

## Sometimes Each Thing has a Different Picture

Like bar charts and block graphs, some pictograms go up instead of across. Sometimes they also have a different picture for each thing.

This one shows how some of Carol's friends get to school each day.

Steam-roller   On foot   Flying saucer   Tortoise back   Monster truck

## These questions will put you in the picture...

Look again at the 2 pictograms on this page, then answer these:
1) How many aardvarks did Harold find on Saturday?
2) How many of Carol's friends go to school by steamroller?

# Line Graphs

## Line Graphs have Lines instead of Bars

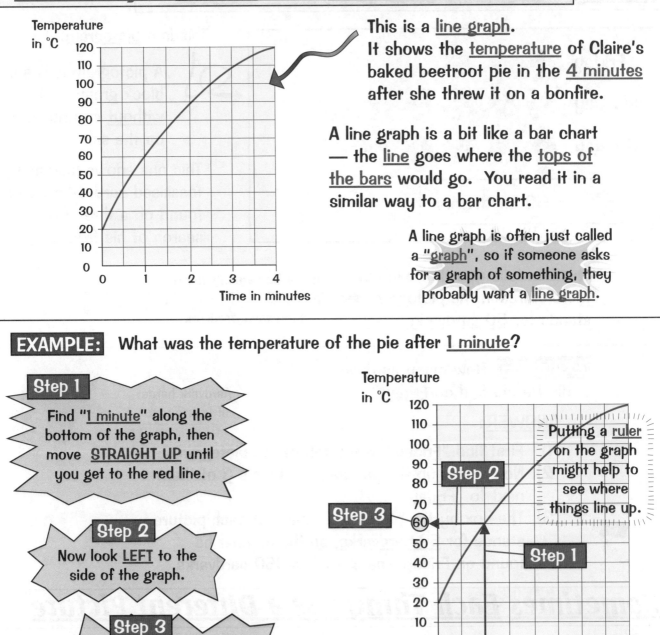

This is a line graph.
It shows the temperature of Claire's baked beetroot pie in the 4 minutes after she threw it on a bonfire.

A line graph is a bit like a bar chart — the line goes where the tops of the bars would go. You read it in a similar way to a bar chart.

A line graph is often just called a "graph", so if someone asks for a graph of something, they probably want a line graph.

**EXAMPLE:** What was the temperature of the pie after 1 minute?

**Step 1**
Find "1 minute" along the bottom of the graph, then move STRAIGHT UP until you get to the red line.

**Step 2**
Now look LEFT to the side of the graph.

**Step 3**
READ OFF the value from the side of the graph.

It says 60 on the side of the graph, so the temperature after 1 minute was 60°C.

Putting a ruler on the graph might help to see where things line up.

You can also read the graph the other way round. You could find when the temperature was 60°C by going across and then down — and you'll see that the time was 1 minute.

## Line Graphs — but there's no point...

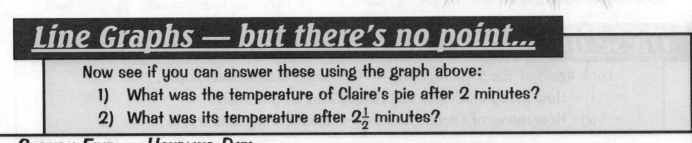

Now see if you can answer these using the graph above:
1) What was the temperature of Claire's pie after 2 minutes?
2) What was its temperature after $2\frac{1}{2}$ minutes?

# Line Graphs

## Drawing Line Graphs — just Join the Crosses

**EXAMPLE:** The table to the right shows the <u>speed</u> of
Zanf the Genie at different <u>times</u> during his last egg
and spoon race. Plot the speeds on a <u>line graph</u>.

| Time | Speed |
|------|-------|
| 30 secs | 21 mph |
| 60 secs | 75 mph |
| 90 secs | 68 mph |
| 120 secs | 33 mph |

Here's how it's done:

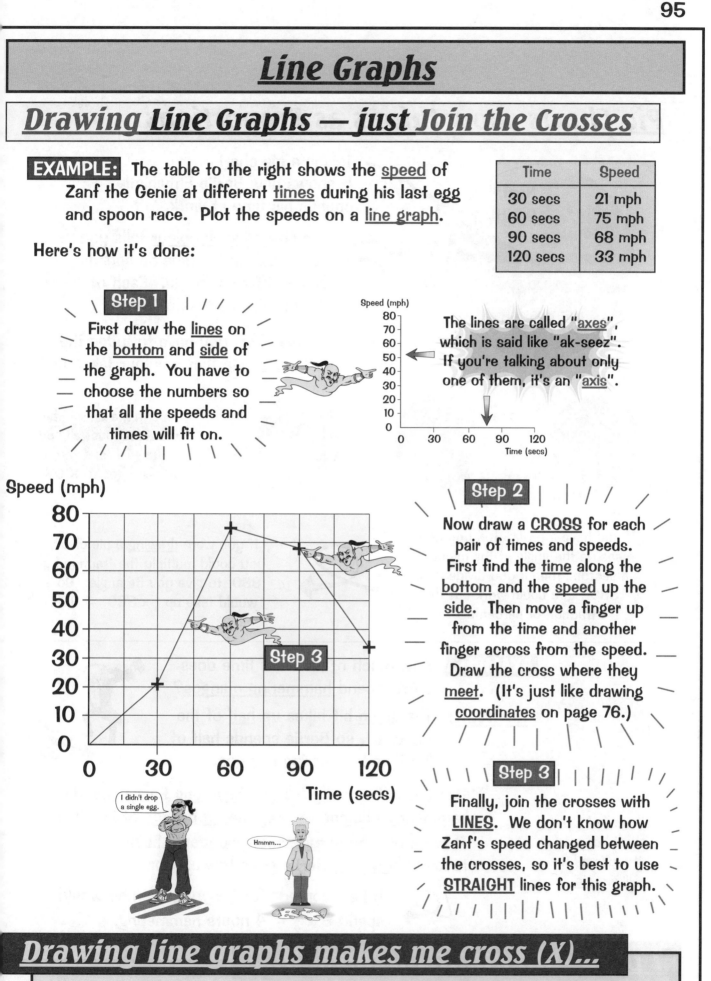

**Step 1**

First draw the <u>lines</u> on
the <u>bottom</u> and <u>side</u> of
the graph. You have to
choose the numbers so
that all the speeds and
times will fit on.

The lines are called "<u>axes</u>",
which is said like "ak-seez".
If you're talking about only
one of them, it's an "<u>axis</u>".

**Step 2**

Now draw a <u>CROSS</u> for each
pair of times and speeds.
First find the <u>time</u> along the
<u>bottom</u> and the <u>speed</u> up the
<u>side</u>. Then move a finger up
from the time and another
finger across from the speed.
Draw the cross where they
<u>meet</u>. (It's just like drawing
<u>coordinates</u> on page 76.)

**Step 3**

Finally, join the crosses with
<u>LINES</u>. We don't know how
Zanf's speed changed between
the crosses, so it's best to use
<u>STRAIGHT</u> lines for this graph.

I didn't drop
a single egg.

Hmmm...

## Drawing line graphs makes me cross (X)...

Now that you've seen how to draw bar charts, pictograms and line graphs, you
could try drawing some of your own. How about a bar chart of hair colour for
your class, or a pictogram of your friends' favourite foods...

# Pie Charts

## Pie Charts show things as Proportions

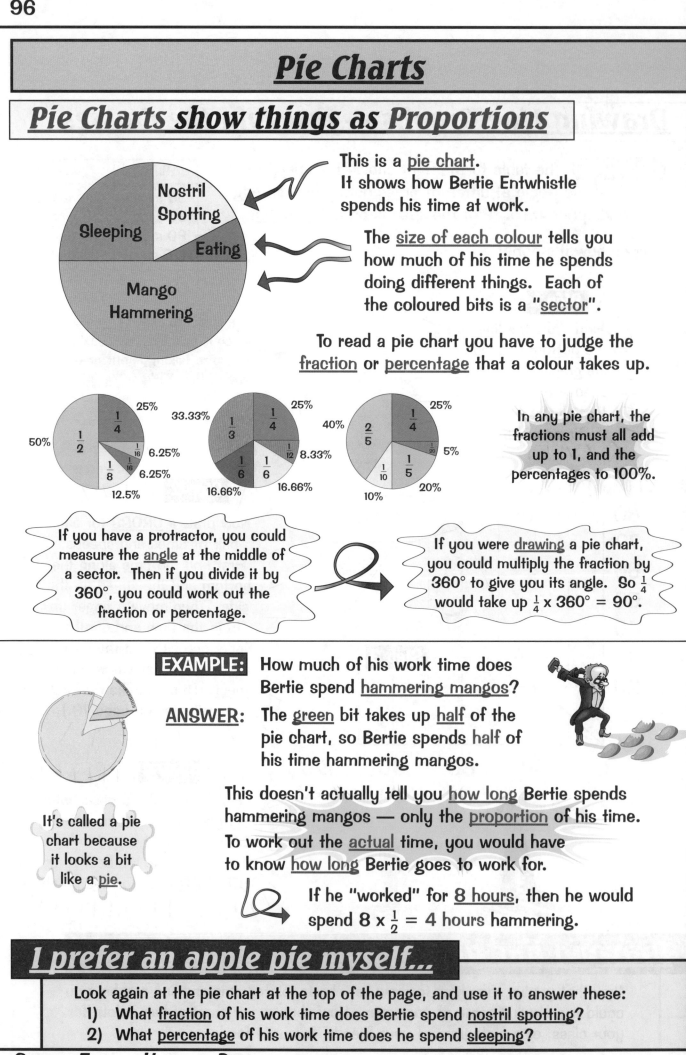

This is a <u>pie chart</u>.
It shows how Bertie Entwhistle spends his time at work.

The <u>size of each colour</u> tells you how much of his time he spends doing different things. Each of the coloured bits is a "<u>sector</u>".

To read a pie chart you have to judge the <u>fraction</u> or <u>percentage</u> that a colour takes up.

In any pie chart, the fractions must all add up to 1, and the percentages to 100%.

If you have a protractor, you could measure the <u>angle</u> at the middle of a sector. Then if you divide it by 360°, you could work out the fraction or percentage.

If you were <u>drawing</u> a pie chart, you could multiply the fraction by 360° to give you its angle. So $\frac{1}{4}$ would take up $\frac{1}{4} \times 360° = 90°$.

**EXAMPLE:** How much of his work time does Bertie spend <u>hammering mangos</u>?

<u>ANSWER:</u> The <u>green</u> bit takes up <u>half</u> of the pie chart, so Bertie spends half of his time hammering mangos.

It's called a pie chart because it looks a bit like a <u>pie</u>.

This doesn't actually tell you <u>how long</u> Bertie spends hammering mangos — only the <u>proportion</u> of his time.
To work out the <u>actual</u> time, you would have to know <u>how long</u> Bertie goes to work for.

If he "worked" for <u>8 hours</u>, then he would spend $8 \times \frac{1}{2} = 4$ hours hammering.

## I prefer an apple pie myself...

Look again at the pie chart at the top of the page, and use it to answer these:
1) What <u>fraction</u> of his work time does Bertie spend <u>nostril spotting</u>?
2) What <u>percentage</u> of his work time does he spend <u>sleeping</u>?

# Understanding Data

## Data Can Be Discrete or Continuous

Discrete data is information that you can count exactly, like the
number of people in the class who have a pet zebra.
Continuous data is information that you can measure to any number
of decimal places, like the height of my zebra — it could be 137 cm,
or 137.16 cm, or 137.16100247 cm. You can never measure it exactly.

**EXAMPLE:** Hubert measured the temperature in his garden at 4 a.m. each morning for
a month. Did he collect continuous data or discrete data?

**ANSWER:** This is continuous data. Even if Hubert rounded his answers to the nearest
degree, the actual temperature could have been measured to any number of
decimal places.

**EXAMPLE:** Sonia recorded the number of goals scored by her football team in each
match last season. Is this continuous data or discrete data?

**ANSWER:** This is discrete data, because the number of goals scored in each match
will always be a whole number — the team can't score a bit of a goal.

## Some Graphs Are Misleading

Sometimes two graphs can look really different, even if they've been drawn using
the same information. If a graph's deliberately drawn in a way that could make
people believe something that's not true, we say it's misleading.

**EXAMPLE:** The graphs below show the number of purple dragons
sold by Judith's Dragon Shop each year for six years.

The second graph makes it look like the sales have increased
much more dramatically than the first one... but the same
numbers have been used to draw both graphs.

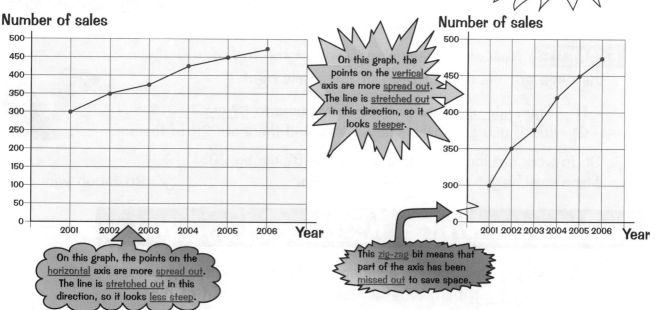

On this graph, the
points on the vertical
axis are more spread out.
The line is stretched out
in this direction, so it
looks steeper.

On this graph, the points on the
horizontal axis are more spread out.
The line is stretched out in this
direction, so it looks less steep.

This zig-zag bit means that
part of the axis has been
missed out to save space.

# Mean, Median, Mode and Range

The mean, median and mode are all types of <u>average</u>.
An average is a number that <u>summarises</u> a load of data.

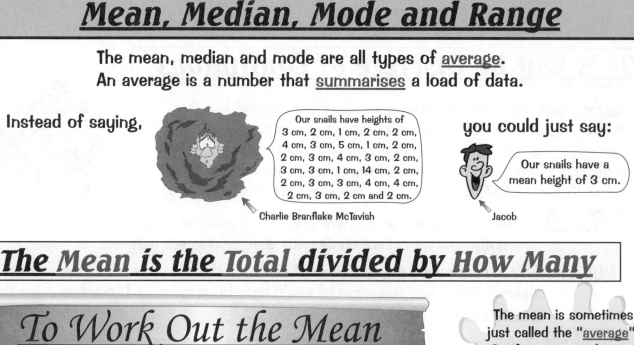

Instead of saying,

Our snails have heights of 3 cm, 2 cm, 1 cm, 2 cm, 2 cm, 4 cm, 3 cm, 5 cm, 1 cm, 2 cm, 2 cm, 3 cm, 4 cm, 3 cm, 2 cm, 3 cm, 3 cm, 1 cm, 14 cm, 2 cm, 2 cm, 3 cm, 3 cm, 4 cm, 4 cm, 2 cm, 3 cm, 2 cm and 2 cm.

Charlie Branflake McTavish

you could just say:

Our snails have a mean height of 3 cm.

Jacob

## The <u>Mean</u> is the <u>Total</u> divided by <u>How Many</u>

### To Work Out the Mean

1) <u>Add up</u> all the numbers.
2) <u>Divide</u> the total by <u>how many</u> numbers there are.

The mean is sometimes just called the "<u>average</u>". So if someone asks you "what's the average of these tiddlywink scores?" then they probably want to know the <u>mean</u>.

**EXAMPLE:** The table below shows the presents bought last Christmas by the four meanest meanies in Millom. What was the <u>mean</u> amount spent by the meanies?

| Present | Cost |
|---------|------|
| A squashed baked bean | 1p |
| A shark-infested aubergine | 4p |
| Two used tea bags | 1p |
| Half a clothes peg | 2p |

### ANSWER:

1) First <u>add up</u> the numbers:
   1p + 4p + 1p + 2p = <u>8p</u>
2) There are 4 numbers, so now you just <u>divide</u> the total by <u>4</u>:
   8p ÷ 4 = 2p.

So 2p was the <u>mean</u> amount spent.

**EXAMPLE:** Now we'll check that Jacob at the top of the page got the mean height of the snails right.

1) If you <u>add up</u> all the heights, they come to <u>87 cm</u>.
2) Now if you <u>count</u> the snails, you'll find there are <u>29</u> of them.

So to work out the mean, you just divide 87 cm by 29:
Mean snail height = 87 cm ÷ 29 = 3 cm.

✓ So Jacob was spot on.

## In the MEANtime, here's a question...

Following a weightlifting accident, Charlie's monster 14 cm snail is now only <u>2 cm</u> tall. What is the new mean height of the snails?

# Mean, Median, Mode and Range

## The Median is the Middle Value

### To Work Out the Median

1) Write all the numbers down in <u>order of size</u>.
2) The number in the <u>middle</u> of your list is the <u>median</u>.

> When there are <u>two</u> <u>middle numbers</u> the median is <u>halfway</u> <u>between</u> them.

**EXAMPLE:**

Dian has the <u>median height</u> in the group because he's in the <u>middle</u> when you arrange them in <u>order of height</u>.

So the <u>median height</u> of the group is 1.8 m.

Me Dian

0.9 m  1.6 m  1.8 m    2.3 m      2.7 m

## The Mode is the Most Common Value

### To Work Out the Mode

1) Write all the numbers down in <u>order of size</u>.
2) Find the <u>number</u> that appears <u>most often</u> in your list. This number is the <u>mode</u>.

> Sometimes there could be <u>more</u> <u>than one</u> mode.

**EXAMPLE:**

The pictogram to the right shows the number of lawns mowed in 10 seconds by the contestants in the South Peckham Superhero Lawn-Mowing Finals.

The number <u>3</u> appears <u>3 times</u>, but <u>1, 5 and 9</u> only appear <u>once</u>. So 3 lawns is the <u>mode</u>.

1      3      3      3      5      9

Denis   Captain   Mightymo   Freddy   Hovermo   Nellie
        Qualcast    Man      Flymore    Hulk

## Wait a MOW, what about these questions...

Dian's group (above) is joined by his half-sister Di, who happens to be <u>0.9 m</u> tall.
1) What is the new <u>median</u> height of the group?
2) What is the <u>mode</u> of their heights?

# Mean, Median, Mode and Range

## The Range is how far from Biggest to Smallest

### To Work Out the Range

1) Write all the numbers down in <u>order of size</u>.
2) Take the <u>smallest number</u> from the <u>biggest number</u>. The answer is the <u>range</u>.

*In other words, the range is the <u>difference</u> between the biggest and smallest numbers.*

**EXAMPLE:**

The pictogram to the right shows how many mountain ranges Frank climbed in each of the last four years.

The <u>biggest number</u> is <u>7</u> and the <u>smallest</u> is <u>2</u>, so:

<u>Range</u> = 7 – 2 = 5 mountain ranges.

range {

**2   4   4   7**

## Ways to Remember Them

<u>Mean</u> — think of the <u>meanies</u>.  Also it's <u>mean</u> because you have to work it out!
<u>Median</u> — remember <u>Dian</u> in the middle with the <u>median</u> height.
<u>Mode</u> — think of the <u>mode</u> of the lawns "<u>mowed</u>".  Also it's the <u>mo</u>st common value.
<u>Range</u> — think of the mountain <u>ranges</u>, or think of it as the <u>difference</u>.

**EXAMPLE:**  The numbers of sprouts juggled by the 8 contestants in this year's Millom Sprout Juggling Contest were 4, 9, 2, 3, 2, 5, 1 and 7.
Find the <u>mean</u>, <u>median</u>, <u>mode</u> and <u>range</u> of these numbers.

<u>ANSWER:</u>  FIRST... put them in order:        1, 2, 2, 3, 4, 5, 7, 9        (✓ still 8)

MEAN $= \dfrac{\text{total}}{\text{how many}} = \dfrac{33}{8} = 4\frac{1}{8} = 4.125$ sprouts.

MEDIAN = the <u>middle</u> value = 3.5 sprouts.   *It's halfway between 3 and 4 because 3 and 4 are both in the middle.*

MODE = <u>mo</u>st common value, which here is simply 2 sprouts.

RANGE = highest number – lowest number = 9 – 1 = 8 sprouts.

Oops!

## Mountain RANGES? They AVERAGES too...

The number of pink igloos in my last 9 dreams were:  5, 10, 16, 3, 8, 11, 0, 10 and 7.
What are the <u>mean</u>, <u>median</u>, <u>mode</u> and <u>range</u> of these numbers?   *Strange dream, that one.*

# Probability

## Probability is how Likely Something is...

Probability is just another way of saying how likely something is.

> 1) If something has a <u>high</u> probability, that means it's pretty <u>likely</u> to happen.
> 2) Something with <u>zero</u> probability will <u>never</u> happen.
> 3) If we say something is <u>certain</u>, that means it <u>will definitely happen</u>.
> 4) We often say things are likely or unlikely. That's another way of saying that something has a <u>high</u> or <u>low probability</u>.

**EXAMPLES:** For example, it's very <u>likely</u> your school will still be there tomorrow, and it's even more likely that the sun will rise tomorrow morning.

On the other hand, it's pretty <u>unlikely</u> that your school will be engulfed by a giant marshmallow, or that the land speed record will be broken by a tortoise.

Don't bet on it!

We say that your school has a <u>high probability</u> of existing tomorrow, but a <u>low probability</u> of being marshmallowed.

## Some Things Are Equally Likely To Happen

We call things with <u>exactly the same chance</u> of happening <u>equally likely</u>.

**EXAMPLE:** Which of these are equally likely?

a) Getting heads, and getting tails, when you toss a normal coin.
b) Rolling a 3, and rolling a 7, when you roll a normal dice.

**ANSWER:** a) These are equally likely. There's <u>the same chance</u> of getting <u>heads</u> as there is of getting <u>tails</u>.
b) These are not equally likely. On a normal dice you can roll <u>1, 2, 3, 4, 5 or 6</u>. So you've got <u>a chance</u> of rolling <u>3</u>, but <u>no chance</u> of getting <u>7</u>.

If things look like they should be <u>equally likely</u>, but turn out not to be, we say the situation is <u>unfair</u>.

**EXAMPLE:** When you roll a <u>normal dice</u>, all the numbers on the dice are <u>equally likely</u> to come up.

Can't we play cards instead?

If you roll a <u>fair dice</u> lots of times, each number will come up about the same number of times. If you roll a dice lots of times, and <u>the same number</u> comes up every time, then it's probably an <u>unfair dice</u>. But to be sure you have to roll it <u>a lot</u> of times — not just 10 or 20, but <u>hundreds</u> or even <u>thousands</u> of times.

# Practice Questions

1) Look at the table to the right, which shows the distances in metres between 4 things. According to the table, how far is it from Cedric's toenail clipping to Kate's house?

| Kate's house | | | |
|---|---|---|---|
| 34 | Cedric's toenail clipping | | |
| 57 | 120 | Theo's secret hamster | |
| 276 | 344 | 217 | Kate's flowerbed |

2) The tallies below show the numbers of different flowers Derek saw the last time he went to his local garden centre.

Tulips   ЖΙ
Daisies   ЖΙ ЖΙ ΙΙ
Triffids   ЖΙ ΙΙΙΙ

a) Draw a frequency table, showing the tallies and their totals.

b) Draw a bar chart showing the numbers of each type of flower he saw.

3) The graph to the right shows the speed of Jerry's banana-powered rocket before it crash-landed 3 seconds after take-off.

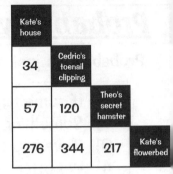

a) How fast was his rocket going after 1 second?

b) How fast was it going after 3 seconds?

4) Richard bought a huge box of tea bags, but next day it was all gone. The pie chart shows the proportion of the teabags each of his friends had used.

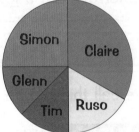

a) Roughly what percentage had Claire used?

b) What else do you need to know to work out how many teabags each person used?

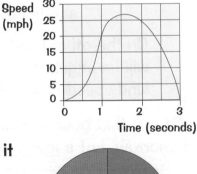

5) The graph on the left was made by the Homework Fan Club using the results of a survey. The club said that the graph proved that homework was much more popular than cake or dogs. Give two reasons why people might say this graph is misleading.

6) Erik the alien measured the lengths of the four fingers on his third hand. The lengths were 8 cm, 23 cm, 8 cm and 7cm. Work out the mean, median, mode and range of his finger lengths.

7) Put the following events in order of how likely they are to happen, from the highest probability to the lowest probability:

Leaves falling from the trees next autumn.
Your teacher turning into a pineapple.
Winning a raffle if you have 1 out of 100 tickets.
Winning a raffle if you have 99 out of 100 tickets.
A tossed coin landing on heads.

Homework
Buy more CGP books

# Words You Need to Know

Here's a list of words that you'll need to know. They haven't all been explained in the book, because it would have got all cluttered up. Read and enjoy...

**2-D** — Flat, like a piece of paper.

**3-D** — Not flat, more like a thick book.

**area** — The amount of surface a shape covers.

**axes** — The lines along the bottom and up the left-hand side of most graphs.

**column** — A column.

**coordinates or co-ordinates** — The numbers on each axis you use to plot a point.

**cuboid** — A solid object like a rectangle, but 3-D.

**diagonal** —

**edge** — It's where 2 faces join.

**equal** — The same in value.

**face** — The flat surface of a solid object.

**horizontal** — Across, on a level.

**opposite** — 2 things are opposite if you can reverse one by doing the other, like + and −.

**parallel lines** — Lines that go in exactly the same direction.

**polygon** — Shape with straight sides.

**reflection** — The same shape, like you'd see it in a mirror.

**rotate** — To turn about a point.

**row** — A row.

**solid** — A 3-D object.

**translation** — The same shape, but moved along, up or down a bit.

**vertex** — The corner where the edges meet.

**vertical** — Upright.

**volume** — The amount of stuff you have... like area, but 3-D.

# Answers

## Section One Answers

Page 4   1) a) one thousand, five hundred and sixteen,
        b) six thousand, eight hundred and twelve,
        c) twenty-five thousand, nine hundred and
          ninety-nine,
        d) thirty-three thousand and forty-one.
      2) 9655    3) 132, 256, 265, 721, 888
      4) 8, 26, 59, 102, 261, 3785, 4600

Page 6   1) 38  2) 99  3) 176  4) 332  5) 412  6) 235  7) 638
      8) 959  9) 1182  10) 1183  11) 1638  12) 2575

Page 8   1) 9  2) 48  3) 151  4) 739  5) 497  6) 76  7) 515
      8) 816     9) a) 83  b) 79  c) 693

Page 11  1) -12°C, -10°C, -6°C, 0°C, 4°C, 7°C
      2) 13°C   3) -10°C
      4) a) -9, b) -5, c) -12, d) -163

Page 14  1) 252  2) 392  3) 832  4) 856  5) 3144  6) 4147

Page 18  1) 121  2) 12  3) 74
      4) 13 remainder 4  5) 24  6) 2566

Page 22  0.08, 0.17, 0.79, 1.03

Page 24  1) a) 780, b) 590, c) 90, d) 30
      2) a) 3600, b) 800, c) 300, d) 23 600
      3) a) 58, b) 12, c) 55, d) 17
      4) a) 2.3, b) 4.6, c) 3.3, d) 9.9, e) 0.8

Page 27  1) a) 1400, b) 871, c) 2500, d) 660
      2) a) 5.6, b) 4.26, c) 1.27, d) 22.2
      3) a) 18, b) 3, c) 52, d) 363, e) 453,
        f) 19, g) 44, h) 132, i) 3340, j) 5335

Page 28  1) 29,  2) 28,  3) 45,  4) 48,  5) 100,  6) 81,
      7) 855,  8) 582,  9) 1495

Page 30  1) Farmhouse (as you would guess — but it isn't
        always what you'd expect).
      2) a) £7.57, b) £16.45, c) £20.97, d) £3.05

Page 31  1) 87 974  2) 252, 253, 265, 723, 997
      3) 12, 53, 142, 153, 352, 635, 2854, 11 452
      4) a) 94, b) 1108, c) 1111   5) a) 9, b) 47, c)673
      6) a) 1215, b) 1508, c) 1932
      7) a) 6 remainder 6, b) 23, c) 327 remainder 2
      8) 4 (so the whole number is 46)   9) 300  10) 12
      11) a) 111.45, b) 0.6
      12) 23.1, 23.11, 23.3, 37.06, 37.6
      13) a) 6000, b) 6447.9, c) 6450, d) 6448
      14) 350  15) a) 0.12, b) 0.2  16) a) 25, b) 78
      17) a) 75, b) 473, c) 776  18) multipack
      19) 1000ml  20) a) 1068p, b) £10.68  21) £ 4.49

## Section Two Answers

Page 32  a) 162    b) 97.9   c) 201.6   d) 24  e) 47.2

Page 34  1) 3/10 x 60, 18   2) 0.4, 0.08, 0.5
      3) 3/10, 43/100, 211/1000

Page 36  1)
      2) 6/9 &2/3,  3/4 & 21/28, 11/55&1/5
      3) 1/3, 2/5, 1/2

Page 37  1) a) 3 1/2, b) 6 1/4, c) 3 3/10, d) 6 2/3, e) 6 6/7
      2) 8 1/5 litres, 8.2 litres

Page 40  1) 8  2) 10%  3) 50%  4) 10

Page 41  1) About 1/2  2) About 25%

Page 42  1) a) 4 to 5, b) 1 to 8  2) 8

Page 44  1)  a) 4, 8, 12, 16, 20, 24, 28, 32, 36, 40,
          44, 48, 52, 56, 60
        b) 9, 18, 27, 36, 45, 54, 63, 72, 81, 90, 99
        c) 36
      2)  a) 1, 2, 3, 6  b) 1, 3, 7, 21  c) 1 and 3

Page 45  1) It ends in a 2, but isn't 2.
      2) A prime is a number with exactly 2 factors
        — 1 and itself.
        Check by working out if it has any factors
        other than 1 and itself.

Page 46  1)  a) 2 × 2 × 2 × 11,  b) 3 × 5 × 5,
        c) 2 × 3 × 3 × 3,  d) 2 × 2 × 2 × 2 × 2 × 3,
        e) 2 × 2 × 3 × 7

Page 47  1) 100, 50, 132  2) 27, 49, 81, 125, 31

Page 48  1) 1, 4, 9, 16, 25, 36, 49, 64, 81, 100
      2) 36, 121, 4, 64  3) 121, 400, 144, 10 000

Page 49  1) -1  2) -5  3) -20  4) -3  5) -3

Page 51  1) a) 41, 45, 49, 77   b) 155, 146, 137, &74
      2) a) 297, 891, 2673 b) 200, 100, 50 c) 21

Page 53  1) add 2   2) a) 12 b) 14

Page 55  It will cost me 23×n to make my easy peasy lemo
        squeezy, which is: T=23×n

Page 56  1) 6         2) 10         3) 90

Page 57  1) 4         2) 9 m         3) 6/12
      4) 1/7, 1/4, 3/8, 98/99, 1 1/2
      5) a) 20 3/4, 20.75, b) 9 3/5, 9.6, c) 6 1/2, 6.5
      6) 1/10 = 0.1, 1/100 = 0.01, 1,
        15/100 (or 3/20) = 0.15, 91/100 = 0.91
      7) a) 40, b) 20, c) 20, d) 18.2
      8) a) about 8/20 or 2/5, b) about 20%
      9) a) 4 to 6, or 2 to 3, b) 5 in 15, or 1 in 3
      10) 7, 14, 21, 28, 35, 42, 49, 56, 63, 70
      11) 1, 2, 4, 7, 14, 28.
        Factor pairs are 1 and 28, 2 and 14, 4 and 7
      12) 2 × 2 × 2 × 7
      13) even: 2, 4, 6, 8, 10  odd: 3, 5, 7, 9
        prime: 2, 3, 5, 7      square: 4, 9
      14) 16, 298
      15) a) 85, b) 162, c)

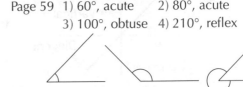

      16) 9 × B  17) 100 + C 18) a) 9, b) 3, c) 2

## Section Three Answers

Page 59  1) 60°, acute      2) 80°, acute
      3) 100°, obtuse   4) 210°, reflex

# Answers

Page 63  2) 12 cm    3) 26 cm
Page 65  1) 15 cm²   2) 3 cm²    3) 14 cm²    4) about 3 cm²
Page 66  e.g.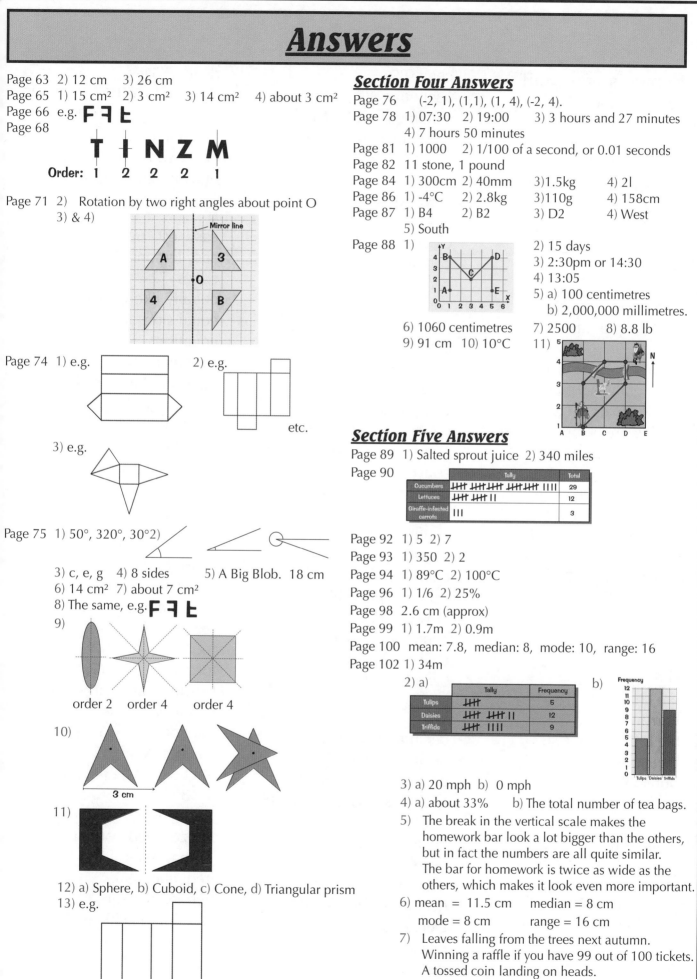
Page 68

Order:  1  2  2  2  1

Page 71  2)  Rotation by two right angles about point O
          3) & 4)

Page 74  1) e.g.                    2) e.g.

                                              etc.

          3) e.g.

Page 75  1) 50°, 320°, 30° 2)

          3) c, e, g   4) 8 sides    5) A Big Blob.  18 cm
          6) 14 cm²  7) about 7 cm²
          8) The same, e.g.
          9)

          order 2     order 4     order 4

          10)

                      3 cm

          11)

          12) a) Sphere, b) Cuboid, c) Cone, d) Triangular prism
          13) e.g.

## Section Four Answers

Page 76       (-2, 1), (1,1), (1, 4), (-2, 4).
Page 78  1) 07:30   2) 19:00      3) 3 hours and 27 minutes
          4) 7 hours 50 minutes
Page 81  1) 1000    2) 1/100 of a second, or 0.01 seconds
Page 82  11 stone, 1 pound
Page 84  1) 300cm  2) 40mm      3)1.5kg       4) 2l
Page 86  1) -4°C    2) 2.8kg      3)110g        4) 158cm
Page 87  1) B4      2) B2        3) D2         4) West
          5) South
Page 88  1)                    2) 15 days
                                3) 2:30pm or 14:30
                                4) 13:05
                                5) a) 100 centimetres
                                    b) 2,000,000 millimetres.
          6) 1060 centimetres    7) 2500        8) 8.8 lb
          9) 91 cm   10) 10°C    11)

## Section Five Answers

Page 89  1) Salted sprout juice 2) 340 miles
Page 90

| | Tally | Total |
|---|---|---|
| Cucumbers | ЖЖ ЖЖЖЖ ЖЖЖЖ IIII | 29 |
| Lettuces | ЖЖ ЖЖ II | 12 |
| Giraffe-infected carrots | III | 3 |

Page 92  1) 5  2) 7
Page 93  1) 350  2) 2
Page 94  1) 89°C  2) 100°C
Page 96  1) 1/6  2) 25%
Page 98  2.6 cm (approx)
Page 99  1) 1.7m  2) 0.9m
Page 100  mean: 7.8,  median: 8,  mode: 10,  range: 16
Page 102 1) 34m

          2) a)

| | Tally | Frequency |
|---|---|---|
| Tulips | ЖЖ | 5 |
| Daisies | ЖЖ ЖЖ II | 12 |
| Triffids | ЖЖ IIII | 9 |

          b)

          3) a) 20 mph  b)  0 mph
          4) a) about 33%      b) The total number of tea bags.
          5)  The break in the vertical scale makes the
              homework bar look a lot bigger than the others,
              but in fact the numbers are all quite similar.
              The bar for homework is twice as wide as the
              others, which makes it look even more important.
          6) mean  =  11.5 cm     median = 8 cm
              mode = 8 cm           range = 16 cm
          7)  Leaves falling from the trees next autumn.
              Winning a raffle if you have 99 out of 100 tickets.
              A tossed coin landing on heads.
              Winning a raffle if you have 1 out of 100 tickets.
              Your teacher turning into a pineapple.

# Index

## Numbers and Stuff

12 hour time  77
24 hour clock  77
3-D shapes  72, 74
3-year-old milk  86
5-metre slug  83
cm  81
kg  81

## A

Ace  33
Ace boxes  57, 73
acute angle  58
adding  5
adding  money  30
adding and subtracting
    decimals  21
adding and subtracting in
    your head  27, 28
adding numbers  5
adding units  82
all clear button  32
angel  58
angles  58, 59
anticlockwise  71
apples  81
areas  64, 65
average  98

## B

bar chart  91
Barrow-on-Sea  39
big blob method  62
bog-snorkelling  30
Boris  87
borrowing  8
brain  87
bread  40

## C

calculator buttons  32, 49
calendar  77
capacity  82
car  81
caterpillar  32

centi  80
centilitres  80
centimetres  80, 81
checking your answer  19
cheesecake  30
clear button  32
clever pigs  27
clocks  77
clockwise  71
columns  79
comparing  42
comparing fractions  36
compass directions  87
con  55
Conan the librarian  78
cone  72
congruence  66
continuous data  97
conversion factors  83
conversion graphs  84
coordinates  76, 87
cost  30
counting on in 10s  2
counting on in 100s  2
counting squares  64
Cow or Spaceship  41
crosses  95
cuboids  72, 74
cute angle  58
cylinder  72

## D

decimal heaven  22
decimal places  24
decimal point  25, 34
decimals  21, 33, 34, 36,
    37, 38, 40
degrees (angles)  58
degrees Celsius  9
delicious chocolate mice  15
denominator  33, 35, 36
Denzel  82
digits  1
discrete data  97
distance tables  89

divider  51
dividing  16, 17, 18, 19, 37
    by 10, 100, 1000: 26
dividing money  30
doing sums in your head  27
drawing line graphs  95

## E

easy  60, 62
easy lemons  55
edges  72
equally likely  101
equal sides  60, 61
equations  54, 55
equilateral  61
equivalent fractions  35, 36
estimating  41
even numbers  47
evening  77
extending the pattern  52

## F

faces  72
factors  44, 46
factor tree method  46
fair  101
false teeth with eyes  12
feet  81, 83
foot  81
formulae  54, 55
fossilised aardvarks  93
fossilised cucumber  30
fraction bars  35, 36
Fraction Man  37
fractions  33, 34, 35, 36,
    37, 41
Frankenstein's monster  67
freeze-dried combine
    harvester  82
frequency  90
frequency tables  90
function machines  56

# Index

**G**

ghosts 92
giant worms 19
goes on forever 9
gone off 86
good old reliable method 78
grams 81
graphs 94
guessing 18

**H**

Haggis Islands 87
hammering mangos 96
heads or tails 101
heavy 81
hedgehog flavour crisps 54
heptagon 61
Herman 87
hexagon 61
hours 77

**I**

inches 81
interpreting graphs 91
into...goes 15
inverses 56
isosceles 61

**K**

Katie the Giant 63
killer hippo 87
kilo 80
kilograms 81, 83
kilometres 81
kilos 81
kitchen scales 85
kites 60
km 81

**L**

last digit 43
leap year 77
length 80, 81
lesser spotted
    Cumbrian Yeti 65

line graphs 94
line symmetry 67
liquids 82
litre 83
litres 82
long division 17
long multiplication 14

**M**

map references 87, 88
maps 87
mashed sprout window cleaner 83
mean 98, 99, 100
measuring angles 58
measuring jugs 85
median 98, 99, 100
metres 80, 83
middle 99, 100
midnight 77
milk 82
milli 80
millilitres 82
millimetres 81
minutes 77
mirror 69
mirror line 67, 69
misleading graphs 97
missing number 20
mixed fractions 33, 34
ml 82
mm 81, 83
mode 98, 99, 100
money 29
money sums 30
multipacks 29
multiples 43
multiplication 12, 13, 14, 25, 27
multiplied by itself 48
multiplier 51
multiplying
    by 10, 100, 1000: 25
    in your head 28
    money 30

**N**

nearest whole number 24
negative numbers 9, 49
nets 73, 74
nostril spotting 96
noughts 4
number line 9, 34, 85
number patterns 50, 51, 52, 53
numerator 33, 35, 36

**O**

obtuse angle 58
octagon 61
octopus 61
odd numbers 47
of 34, 43
one is not a prime number 45
opposites 8, 16, 19, 56
order of rotational symmetry 68
ordering decimals 22
ordering negative numbers 10
ordering numbers 2, 3
ounces 81

**P**

parallel lines 60
parallelograms 60
patterns 50, 51, 52, 53
penguins 9
pentagon 61
percentages 38, 39, 40, 41
perimeters 62, 63
perims 63
perpendicular lines 60
pickled turnip 82
pictograms 93
picture patterns 52
pie charts 96
pints 82, 83
plus/minus button 32, 49
point of rotation 71
points 76
polygons 61
pounds 81, 84

# *Index*

press the wrong button 49
previous term 51
prime factors 46
prime numbers 45
prism 72
probability 101
proportions 42, 96
protractor 58, 59
purple donkey 84
pyramid 72, 74

**Q**
quadrilaterals 60

**R**
racing hamster 30
radioactive sprouts 52
range 100
ratios 42
rattlesnake roll 57
reading graphs 84
reading maps 87
reading scales 85, 86
reading timetables 79
rectangles 60
reflection 69
reflex angle 58
regular polygons 61
remainder 15, 37
rhombus 60
ridiculous maths word 66
right angle 58
right-angled triangle 61
rise in temperature 11
roast beans 33
rotate 68, 71
rotational symmetry 68
rounding 23
rounding off to
     decimal places 24
rows 79
ruler 81, 86

**S**
scalene 61
scales 85
seconds 77
sector 96
sequences 50, 51, 52, 53
shape nets 74
shapes 60, 61, 72
sharing 15
short division 16
short easy stages 78
sides 60, 61
sliding 70
slime 86
slug 83
snails 80
sneaky tricksters 36
space 82
sphere 72
spoons 82
sprouts 52, 53
spruce juice 82
square numbers 48
square root button 32
squares 60
squashed cucumbers 80
stones 81
subtracting 7
subtracting money 30
subtracting units 82
Sumo Hamster 87
superheroes 23
symmetry 67, 68

**T**
tables 89
tablespoon 82
taking away 7
tally marks 90
teaspoon 82
temperature changes 11
terms 51
tetrahedron 72
The Space Boys 75
thermometers 11, 85

time 77, 78, 79
times by itself 48
times tables 13, 43, 47
timetables 79
tonne 83
total cost 54, 55
tracing paper 67, 70
tracks 81
translation 70
trapezium 60
triangle 61, 64
triangular prism 72, 74
turning 67, 71

**U**
unfair 101
units 80, 81, 82

**V**
value for money 29
vertices 72
volume 82

**W**
wasp truffles 42
weight 81
where you are 87
whole number answers 19
winner of the race 78
wooooooing noises 92
word formulae 54, 55
worms 53

**X**
x-coordinate 76

**Y**
y-coordinate 76
YTS 19

**Z**
Zanf the Genie 95
zapf dingbat 86
zebra 97
zeros 25